Becoming

Positively

Awesome

Transform Your Life Through the Power of Positive Thinking

By: Drs. Darren & Kelley Kirchner, Dr. Scott Butler, Kari Whitaker, Dr. Jeffrey J. Rodman, Jerry Barnett, Aloha McGregor, Kiersten Blest, Lura J. Dahlem, Aruna Ramamurthy, Tracie Ullman, Lisa Ann Studer, Michelle Duffy, Julee Muro de Gerome, Amanda Scott, Helen Fong, John Jaco, Roselito De Los Reyes, Mischa Holt, Elizabeth Garvey, Michael Stevenson

April 27, 2023

Edited by: Elizabeth Garvey

Becoming Positively Awesome

Table of Contents

"Positive thinking will let you do everything better than negative thinking will."

Zig Ziglar

Introduction

Michael Stevenson MNLP, MTT, MHt

If there's one thing most humans struggle with, it's living up to the lofty standards we have in our minds.

"I'm not attractive enough."

"I'm not smart enough."

"I'm not well enough off."

"I'm not successful enough."

"I'm not good enough."

And the list goes on.

I've been a professional Clinical Hypnotherapist, Success and Life Coach, and Neuro-Linguistic Programming Master Practitioner and Master Trainer starting nearly a quarter of a century ago. During that time, I've worked with countless people and seen the "human condition" up close.

But not nearly as close as I have in my own life.

Long before I began my personal journey to *Becoming Positively Awesome*, when I was born in February 1973, my mom was just 14 years old and a few months shy of graduating from junior high school.

Times were different back then. When a girl got pregnant, she was shuttled away in shame and hidden from the rest of the teenage population. She was a pariah. A degenerate.

Perhaps this is where my initial self-esteem issues began, as a baby in the womb, feeling the feelings of a scared little girl who was told that she was worthless.

Not only was my mother young—a child herself—but she was also afflicted with a vicious personality disorder: Borderline Personality Disorder.

My father, an 18-year-old junior in high school, wanted nothing to do with me.

Between my grandparents' desire to provide a healthy environment and hold reasonable boundaries and my mother's tumultuous mood swings, things came to a head when my mother was 17 and I was just three. My mother packed up all our belongings into two suitcases and bought a one-way Greyhound ticket to get away from my grandparent's rules. My life took a dramatic turn for the worse.

I was no longer sheltered by the normalcy of my grandparents' loving, nurturing home, and the next 16 years of my life were a tumultuous, unbearable, living hell.

I survived neglect, abuse, and even natural disasters, but it all took a toll on me. By the time I was 18 years old, I was bitter, untrusting, angry, shy, and withdrawn to the point of being almost anti-social.

By 19, I had made a series of decisions that accelerated my downward spiral and had me homeless, living on the streets, for around six months.

My life felt like a living tragedy. I felt stupid, poor, ugly, worthless, and unlovable. I felt like I had nowhere to turn.

Luckily, through the help of a dear friend, I got reconnected to my grandparents and got the hand up I needed to get off the streets and back on my feet.

I thought differently once I got off the streets. I had hit a bottom so deep, I never wanted to go back there again. For the first time in my life, I started focusing on feeling better about myself and about my life.

First, I began focusing on mindset, pulling from some visualization exercises that I learned as a teenager, and then beginning to read books to better myself.

I achieved a bit of success over the next few years with my new focus, but I still had a lot of negative effects from my past. I still had self-esteem issues, a crippling shyness, and some bad habits that I just couldn't seem to kick.

One of those bad habits was smoking. I was hopelessly addicted to cigarettes, smoking as much as three packs—that's 60 cigarettes—in a day.

I had tried everything for years to quit, from cold turkey to patches to medication, but nothing seemed to help. That addiction was the strongest thing I had ever encountered in my life, and I felt completely defeated.

Other people would say, "Just quit!" They would talk about things like "will power," but I felt like I had none.

Then, one day in August 1998, I was at the annual county fair with my friends. We made this trip each year to see one of my favorite shows in the world: the comedy hypnosis show.

Each year, I would go multiple times to watch the stage hypnotist. Now, mind you, I didn't believe in hypnosis. I thought what was happening on stage was ridiculously funny… but also just ridiculous.

I figured the people on stage were actors, or gullible, or maybe even just drunk.

Despite what we see in these entertainment shows, the clinical use of hypnosis, called hypnotherapy, is very real, as is your subconscious mind. Modern hypnotherapy was created by a licensed medical doctor, Dr. James Braid, and is scientifically validated.

At the end of the show, just for fun, I purchased three hypnosis tapes: improve your memory, improve your psychic ability, and quit smoking.

A few weeks later, on a night with nothing good on TV, I thought, *"What the heck?"* I put on the quit smoking tape and drifted off to sleep, and my life changed forever.

I woke up the next morning, September 6th, 1998, and never touched another cigarette again. Instantly, cigarettes disappeared from my life, and I never had a single craving or withdrawal.

I was fascinated and so intensely curious, that I have dedicated the following 25 years of my life to understanding the subconscious mind and helping people change their lives through tools like hypnotherapy and Neuro-Linguistic Programming.

I found that, while most people don't believe in hypnosis, we have all been hypnotized.

We came here into this world with unlimited potential, holistic intentions, and nothing but pure love for ourselves and others. But then the circumstances of life hypnotize us into believing lies such as:

"I'm not attractive enough."

"I'm not smart enough."

"I'm not well enough off."

"I'm not successful enough."

"I'm not good enough."

And the list goes on.

While some have called me one of the best hypnotists on the planet, most often, I'm actually de-hypnotizing people.

When I was homeless, I felt completely worthless and didn't feel I had anything to contribute to the world. This is why, the first time Les Brown pointed at my heart and said, "There's greatness within you!" I broke down in tears.

You are magnificent. And if you already know it, you're more magnificent than you already know.

The chapters that follow in this book will help you clear that rubble that life has built up around your soul, the "junk" that makes you feel negativity in your life, and helps you become positively awesome.

It is no easy feat wrangling twenty authors together around one common message. But this message is easy, because each of them has undergone their own journey to *Becoming Positively Awesome*, and each is helping others to become positively awesome in their lives as well.

I know you will love this book as much as I do.

Michael Stevenson
Transform Destiny
April 2023

Creating a Momentum of Accomplishment

Drs. Darren & Kelley Kirchner

So many people live lives of average momentum. They are on a rollercoaster, trudging up through the week to get to the weekend, then flying down with all the speed and excitement. Only to trudge up the next hill on Monday. Their purpose is to make it through the week and have enough money after they pay the bills to have a little fun.

Other people seem to run forward like an airplane gaining speed to take off and soar. They seem to go through life with ease and flow. Success and abundance follow them.

Most people never climb off the rollercoaster to look around and choose another way. They may look at the lifestyles of successful people and wonder how they got lucky, or why this isn't happening to them, but they don't take the steps to change their destinies.

Momentum is happening all around us and to us in our lives every day. Every small, seemingly unimportant action has a result, and those results build momentum.

Are these actions building momentum towards health, towards loving relationships, towards peace, and towards abundance? Or are they taking us towards the mediocrity of poor health, unfulfilling relationships, a sarcastic and biased approach towards others, and the constant desperation of lack?

You are already choosing with your actions. And the good news is that no matter what direction your actions have been taking you, you can choose a new course. The difference between the people stuck on the rollercoaster's ups and downs, and the people who are making their way down the runway towards flight is the course corrections they make.

It takes a moment to decide that your life will change for the better. The choice is yours.

Every moment is a choice. When actions build up, we call that momentum. In every moment, you can make a choice, take one action, and start building a momentum of accomplishment.

During a spiritual retreat, we were asked to meditate on the concept that every moment in life is perfect.

"I struggled with this idea throughout the retreat." Darren says. His idea of perfection was fixed and unchangeable.

Finally, he went to the teacher and asked to have this idea clarified. The teacher explained that the word "perfect" may be an imprecise translation and that a better term could be, "Every moment in life is complete. It contains all we need, lacks nothing, and therefore, there is no reason to delay."

There is no reason to delay our progress, our growth, our actualization... our momentum.

We all contain all the resources that we may need to live our best lives in every moment. In fact, what is life but a collection of moments?

In the most universal sense, we are always, at all times, in control of the life we create. The only real choice we have is in the moment, to acknowledge that truth and live by it.

We can sum many of the great truths in life up as binary options, a choice between two polar ideas. Western philosophy has theory and practice. Eastern philosophy has yin and yang. Science has positive and negative polarities. Time is made up of days and nights. These choices are seemingly everywhere we look.

We can also see the moments of life as a binary choice between *Will* and *Whim*. Whichever state we choose is like a window into our life, shaping and defining our perception of our reality. When we are at *a whim*, we see the moment as outside our control. Our choices seem limited. We are like a leaf in the wind. When we operate from a perspective of *will*, we are in control of our world. We see the moment as full of possibilities. We are not only the leaf and the wind, but the very forces of Nature that created both!

What is *not* possible from such a perspective?

Our highest aspirations and visions are only a series of moments away. The simple act of choosing to assume your nature virtually assures that you will get what you choose to focus on. So, focus on what you want.

You've focused on and decided what you want. Now, how do you get there?

Momentum Requires Movement

To kick start momentum, it is necessary to take a real-world action. Planning is useful and has an important place in achieving outcomes, but don't let it steal your momentum. We've all known people who were stuck in limbo, scared to make a choice, and missing out on experiences because of it.

You'll find that momentum begins when actions are taken. We measure progress in actions, not thoughts. Ask yourself, what is one action you can take now, which, looking back on it later, will have gotten the ball rolling?

Decide on something small and do it. What is the next step you can take? If you don't see the next step, then you haven't broken it down enough. When you are feeling like you can't take the next step, ask yourself, is this one step, or do I need to break it down more? When you know you can take the step, you've broken it down enough.

For example, you may think that the next step in a project is to make a phone call. But when you get ready to make the call, you realize you don't have all the details together to get the information you need during the call. The next step is to make a few notes to prepare for the phone call.

Sometimes, there are two choices that feel right, and we can feel frozen in inaction, not knowing which action to take. The good news is that if you have two good options, you can choose either. Remember, they are both good choices. Simply make a choice and move forward.

After you've taken action, it's time to let the results of your actions build momentum.

Every action has a result. Usually, that result is towards your outcome, or not towards it. When the result is towards your outcome, take a moment to feel good about it... and then take another action. (Feeling good about your outcome is an important part of building momentum — don't skip this step!)

Maybe your result wasn't what you wanted. Don't let it slow you down. A momentum of accomplishment is not defined by any one act, result, or choice, but by the accumulation of them. This momentum builds when we learn from our results and move forward, anyway.

So, when the result is not what you wanted, stop to think about what you can learn from the result. Decide what to do differently and do it. Then take a moment to feel good about it.

Having a strategy of learning from our results and changing our actions to account for them is something that will supercharge your momentum. Feel good about it!

One Simple Way to Practice Building Momentum

Here is one simple thing that can be done daily, without taking too much time, that will have profound results on your focus, and therefore, your results. That is to take control of one thing.

Most things can seem out of your control. Take control of one thing in your life that you have absolute control over. For instance, the time you wake in the morning may be because of your job. You don't have to choose the last moment possible to drag yourself out of bed and rush to get there on time. Instead, you can choose to wake up with extra time, refreshed, and looking forward to your day. You can choose what you'll think about and activities you can accomplish first thing to set the course for your day.

Choose When and How You Wake Up

There are many ways to be in control of when and how you wake up every day. Here are a few examples of how to accomplish taking control of how you wake up:

Set a Purpose

Take time every night before bed to set a purpose for the following day. Setting this purpose before bed allows your subconscious mind to contemplate the purpose through the night and will often allow it to trigger ideas the following day, moving you closer to your outcomes. It also means that when you wake up in the morning, you'll have a reason to get out of bed and get started. Most people notice quickly that they have renewed energy from this simple exercise.

Access a High State and Energy Level

Another way is to set yourself up to be at the highest perspective and energy level you can maintain. One of the highest states that is readily available to everyone is that of gratitude.

Gratitude Exercises

Gratitude exercises allow us to appreciate the good things in our lives and help us recognize the blessings we have, which

16

can lead to increased feelings of joy, contentment, and overall happiness. We can remind ourselves that even small moments of joy can be savored and appreciated. By building a positive outlook on life, enabling us to better handle difficult times and focusing on the good, we are telling our subconscious mind that this is the track we choose. We are training our brain to fire the brain cells that lead to happiness and fulfillment.

So, write three things you are grateful for today and why. Reflect on how much these moments mean to you and how they enrich your life. This also works wonderfully as a contemplation exercise.

1. For Someone: Think of someone who has had a positive impact on your life and take a few moments to appreciate them. Write at least three things that they have done for you or qualities they possess, which make them special to you.
2. For Something: Reflect on something in your life that you are thankful for. It can be a material possession, an experience, or anything else that brings you joy or comfort. Write at least three ways in which this thing has improved your life and why it means something to you.
3. For a Character Trait: Think of someone who has a character trait that you admire and take a few moments to appreciate it. It can be someone you know or a famous person, for example. Write at least three ways in which this character trait has enriched your life and why it is important to you.

Take the time to reflect on these things and appreciate them fully. This will help cultivate an attitude of gratitude that will elevate your life and build on your momentum of accomplishment.

Remember, the idea is to take control of one thing. You don't have to do all these suggestions; you can pick any of them and make it the one thing you are in control of. Pick one and see what results it brings in your life. If it doesn't bring the results you want, try another, and another. One secret is to start, and don't stop.

By taking actions, reflecting on the results, making new plans, and feeling good about it, you are training your subconscious mind to look for ways to build momentum. You are also training your brain to build the pathways to make this all easier.

Soon, you'll be above each individual project, each with its own momentum, and you'll see that you are living a lifestyle of momentum of accomplishment. You'll be soaring like that airplane that worked so hard to get off the ground, and now the wheels are up, and you are in control over the pilot's seat of your life.

The key to unlocking our greatest potential and living our best life is within each of us. By choosing to focus on what we want in life and taking the actions needed to get there, we can tap into our own momentum of accomplishment and make it a reality. No matter the direction our past choices have taken us, by committing to mindful action and purposeful will, we can always start anew. Every moment is a choice, and that choice is simply to take an action that moves you forward. By doing so, we set ourselves on the path to creating the life of our dreams. With discipline, commitment, and courage to take control of our lives in each present moment, the possibilities are infinite. Go forth and make it happen!

The power is yours!

About Drs. Darren & Kelley Kirchner

Drs. Darren & Kelley Kirchner are the Founders and Lead Educators of Natural Solutions Group. They specialize in restoring and maintaining all aspects of health (Mind/Body/Spirit) through the most natural means available.

The doctors have extensive experience in natural medicine and have helped people restore their health, from all walks of life and all corners of the globe. They are experienced in providing quality education, innovative solutions, and a personalized approach to patient care. Their approach and methods are sought by natural providers and their clients from across the country.

Drs. Darren and Kelley are committed to providing the highest level of services and programs to patients and their providers. They are passionate about helping people find optimal health and wellness through natural methods. They are dedicated to helping people achieve their health goals and live their best lives.

For free resources to help you build a Momentum of Accomplishment, visit www.BPABook.com/gift/Darren-Kelley

The Only True Prison Is the One Between Your Ears

Dr. Scott Butler

Have you ever felt trapped or stuck in your life, like everyone or everything was against you? That no matter what happens, life just doesn't get better? That's the personal prison you've created.

I call it that because when described this way; it feels dark and hopeless, like a prison. I hope you are reading this because you are ready to acknowledge your prison, your part in it, and you are ready to change it.

You've heard the phrases:

> "You are the master of your own destiny."

> "Only you hold the keys to your future."

> "Life is what you make it."

> … and many more just like these.

And while they may give you a short-term boost of excitement, or even a little hope, rarely will you use them to create change. How often do you see social media posts that share messages like these? Most of the time, you feel good for a few seconds.

I'll share a little secret with you. After a while, they would piss me off. Because I didn't understand how these quaint little quotes worked in real life. And I would just get angry at

21

the absurdity of people saying that I could create the life I wanted. Life isn't that simple, right?

I didn't understand how to create the life I wanted. I thought life happened, and it was my job to deal with it. The challenges I encountered were because I had the life I earned, deserved, and was supposed to live.

You say you want change, something better or different. The reality is that you use tools like complacency and fear rather than hope, willingness, and effort to create your life. That's a dead-end path.

First things first, every emotion and every thought process serves you, so being happy, proud, and grateful for ALL your tools is essential. Complacency, for example, can serve you. The trick is deciding if, when, and for how long. So, first be grateful for ALL the unique experiences in life and ALL the ways you have of processing those experiences because they serve you.

I've gotten pushback on this advice because it's tough to be grateful for the pain and challenges you face, but those experiences can be used to your advantage if you so choose. Consistent gratitude in your life is a lot like consistent sunshine on plants. The more you have, the more things grow and flourish.

Being grateful for the bad, and the not so pretty in your life, is just as important as being grateful for beauty and goodness, because they all give you the tools you need to move forward.

You now know complacency is a tool. Is it the tool that gets you out of the prison of your own making? Most likely not. So, your answer is to find and use other tools, and that includes finding guidance and mentorship.

The next step in letting yourself out of the prison you've created is to realize you are the one who created it. Not your parents, teachers, boss, or spouse, regardless of their actions and behaviors. It's not "life's fault" either.

This is rarely a fun conversation to have. Most of the time, you'll want to blame other people and circumstances in times of strife and challenge. It's easier to say "he/she did this or that, or the unplanned happened, and that's why my life is the way it is". It's easy to forget that you are the one that had or kept them in your life, you are the one that valued their behaviors, you are the one who allowed events or other's actions to dictate how you think, believe, act, and ultimately live.

This is where we talk about the key to unlocking that door to your cell. The moment you conclude that all things that influence your life are there because you choose for them to be there is when that key magically appears. It appears because that is when you become empowered.

This is a word that gets thrown around a lot in today's world. It usually references someone standing up and yelling their personal beliefs and then claiming they finally have the strength to do so because they are finally empowered. However, as you look closer, it's all too common that what you see is an individual who is claiming empowerment because they are blaming other people or things for their problems.

True empowerment comes from when you look inside and realize you are the one that is responsible for your problems.

STOP!!!!! Right now!

Here is where you may start either fighting the conversation or start beating yourself up, neither is helping you. Instead, use this moment to realize that if you can take on the knowledge that all things in your life are there because you chose them, then that means that everything from this moment on is going to be in your life because you choose it. Friends, family, career, love, adventure, and whatever else you select to have in your life.

Did you hear the lock click open or was that just me?

Where do you go from here? You are grateful for everything in your life. You now realize that everything that's in your life is because you put it there, and you are empowered by this knowledge.

So, what's next? That depends on you. What is it you want and will create? Something I earnestly hope with all my heart is that you understand more quickly and with more resolve and enthusiasm than I did, is that whatever you will create will occur as quickly and effortlessly as you choose.

Becoming who you want to be and where you want to be should probably start with who are you now and where have you come from. Do not use this step as the place to replay all the bad things that have occurred in your life. Rather, use this step as a time that you objectively look at your life and can say this is my path that I became who I am. This is what I will change to become who I want to be.

Remember to be grateful for the choices that you've made to become who you are. Otherwise, you wouldn't be here now, reading this chapter written specifically for you to create better for yourself.

Now to touch on some of the more common ways that you keep yourself in a cell, and how to influence them.

1. Allowing the anchors you placed in your life to keep you tethered to a specific spot. This will include how you see yourself, how you believe you are supposed to live, and choosing to believe that all you have now is all you deserve. Finding the way to cut those anchors loose is the only way you will move from that spot.

2. Not knowing what it is you really want in your life. Have you noticed that when asked what it is you want in your life that you aren't able to give a specific, comprehensive list? You can, however, enumerate what you don't want. You must start this adventure knowing where it is you want to go, not where you don't want to go. Where do you want to go?

3. You look outside of yourself for those things that you believe are keeping you trapped and the resources you need to be freed. In reality, they come from inside of you. Just like how you created your current cell, you have the tools to free yourself.

You may not know how to use those tools immediately, and that's when you seek help from those who have walked these paths successfully. When you look outside, ask yourself questions to shift your focus.

Here are a few examples. Use the approach, not the specific questions:

"I don't have the money."	What is something I can do to earn that capital until I can create what I want specifically!
"I don't have the time."	How much time do I spend on social media, tv, and video games every day?
"I don't know how to talk to people about my business." "I don't know how to do this."	Are there any free online or in person classes that will teach me how to do this until I can afford to take more advanced training?
"My significant other says this…"	Do they know how important this is to mine & our future? Do I need to make this decision based on their opinion?

It comes to a place of using your recently discovered empowerment to your benefit.

4. You are unwilling to put in the work, effort, actions, behaviors, and sacrifice that it takes to create the life you want. Wanting something and being willing to change everything, including and especially yourself, are two different things.

A behavior that you most likely use in your life is saying you want something different or better and then you act as if you can create change using the same behavior that created your current cell. Different results require different approaches. Once you decide what it is you want in your life, the next step is being willing to get it and be committed.

The last piece of advice I want to share is that you may very well get frustrated, tired, or angry at creating what you want because of the resistance that you come up against. Resistance creates knowledge, strength, and endurance. Many of life's critical lessons come from resistance.

Moving forward, it's important to remember that you can change the path as long as you're creating the result you want. Your goal can remain somewhat rigid while the path to it is more flexible.

Recently I was having a conversation about the lives people have and it was said that people have the lives that they want. I said people have the lives that they believe they deserve, the lives they believe that they have earned, and the result is the lives that they have created.

These are the questions to ask yourself to open the door to your current prison and to create the existence you want:

Do I believe I have the life I deserve?

Do I believe I have the life I have earned?

Do I have the life I want?

Who am I?

Who do I want to be?

What is the life I want to create?

Who and what can I look to for help and guidance?

What am I willing to change to the get the answers I want?

Your prison is your creation. Your life is your total and complete creation. You can keep yourself in a life that you aren't happy with or you can put yourself in a life that you get what you want. The greatest challenges you encounter will come from you. The greatest satisfaction and successes you experience will also come from you. Which are you going to choose?

About Dr. Scott Butler

 Scott Butler is a highly experienced physician, who has been in practice for 22 years and holds a Doctorate in Chiropractic, certification in acupuncture, hypnotherapy & coaching, from Logan University & Transform Destiny. His career is driven by his passion, focus and efforts to help those whose lives are out of balance, by using combinations of physical, mental, energetic, and emotional care.

Dr. Butler is an avid learner and teacher. He regularly attends and presents at conferences and seminars to stay up to date on the latest techniques and treatments. He also offers online education to help people take their health and well-being into their own hands and to the next level.

Dr. Butler is dedicated to providing quality care and helping his patients and clients reach their goals.

To get Scott's gift, visit:
www.BPABook.com/gift/Scott

Tiny Matters

Kari K. Whitaker, NLPMP, MTT, MHt, MSC, EFT
In Memory of Greg "Pinky" Williams

It is a question often pondered... What's the meaning of life? My life? If we backtrack a bit, I can recall feeling restless and tired, you know- BURNED OUT! I was not fulfilled inside.

So why not? I had a great career as a Realtor®. My husband Wade and my parents wholeheartedly supported me. I had a home I loved in a city and community I enjoyed and can recall many of my favorite memories, like venturing into Mud Creek Park behind our house, to explore and connect with these big questions.

This was a public park that no one except a very few neighbors and dog walkers used. The best part about it was it's raw, rustic, and untampered. The park had these fabulous old wild overgrown trails in a canyon waterbed that was now dry.

It was wonderful because my yellow lab, Jack, could roam off leash and we could see the wild deer, rabbits, hawks, and the occasional coyote or fox. My time there was blissful, and it's the times when I felt happiest. I would talk out loud to all the nature like a fool and ask the big questions... what am I supposed to be doing with my life and time here?

I take everything too seriously and my husband reminds me to take a breath and just BE- without all my expectations and agendas. It's brilliant advice in theory and difficult for me to do. And somehow out in nature's wonder, I feel creative, alive, connected.

So, on a walk one day, I was taking it all in and thinking about what it all means and realized that I do not really need any substantive answers. I simply needed to listen to the nudge and the callings that I felt inside. The chatter was still there, only quieted a little and was further away. It was this intuitiveness that created my next decision and career move.

Many years earlier, while practicing real estate, I had followed the guidance of hiring a coach. Because my business coach was so helpful and instrumental in my growth in career and life, I now desired to be a coach, too. This seemed like a natural way to evolve self-discovery plus realize fulfillment and meaning simultaneously.

Helping serve others with their challenges and roadblocks would be a worthy pursuit. Here is where I will insert life learning number one: You can get where you want to go faster and easier sometimes if you're vulnerable and courageous enough to ask for help.

My personal program had always been figuring it out- make it happen- to be resourceful Kari! I took a different approach and had lunch with Craig, the most fabulously supportive broker/owner any real estate office could have.

He organized lunch for me with the office productivity coach, Steve. One of Craig's superpowers is to see potential in people, and he is constantly creating opportunity and collaboration for those around him. This lunch could foster and support all as individuals and create a team that could partner together on the mission of transforming lives in our office.

I was thrilled and excited and clueless about what it might entail or look like because we had discussed no details specifically. And anyone who knows me knows…. details are necessary!

Shortly after our successful lunch meeting, I receive a text message one afternoon that said something like… could you cover my 90-minute group session tomorrow? I had panicked reading this as all the self-doubt and overflow of how and why questions started racing through my mind. What will I say? I have no experience. I do not know the structure. The people? What topic or messaging? Me?

WAIT! STOP IT! Now my inner voice recognized the runaway brain train and yelled out, THIS is an opportunity!! Just type three easy letters Y… E… S as quickly as possible. Now, before you think too far and land at a NO! You asked for this- GO.

 And so, I did type YES and then proceeded with a minor freak out and limiting belief story for a few hours. The result was everything imagined- electric, empowering, fulfilling, motivating, inspiring and full of discomfort all at the same time. I knew I had found a space I wanted to stay in for a while and this felt awesome.

Fast forward to New Year's Eve at our favorite spot- Wade's family ranch in North Texas. This is a place where neighbors are sparse, and cows are aplenty. A quiet place for recuperation, unwinding, and chilling time; however, you please.

On the early morning of January 1, 2020, with a cup of coffee in hand, I sat on the long porch in the rocker chair overlooking the serenity and calm of the pasture, contemplating in my journal what life might look like if we moved here. And I did a thorough job of drafting out and answering all the hard questions.

I mean, could I leave the real estate practice I had built and worked so hard on? And what about country life? Living with more cows than people? What would we do? How could we make a living? And what about sushi night?

No, but for real I did a deep dive on all the things. And surprisingly, it was very simple for me. Because when you KNOW inside, you really know. See, life had been a rat race of keeping up with more and more, and the nonsense of it all had reached a peak for me.

A harsh and tragic truth had made contemplating this decision quite clear for me. That previous summer I had sat on this same porch on a different gorgeous morning overlooking beauty and the start of a new day. Quiet, but not alone that morning.

I had the gift of having a private personal moment with my brother-in-law, who we call Pinky. He had this strange nickname because he was so fairly complected and like me he could turn bright pink with emotion. Per usual on this morning, Pinky was up before dawn. He had always kept a busy schedule dedicated to his work and career at International Paper.

Pinky was the funniest person I knew. He was always seeing that everybody felt comfortable and had what they needed to feel good. He had a huge laugh that was contagious and bold. I will relish that private morning as I recall him vulnerable and worried and saying to me...... I just hope it's not brain cancer- he had just lost a friend to that outcome, he said. In the weeks ahead, they made the diagnosis- brain cancer.

All our hearts were hurting as this vibrant and young man of only 56 was facing the end. I cannot imagine his loss of not experiencing the joys of his children married or his hard work paying off with a glorious retirement shared with his wife, Traci. Agonizing sadness, as too many know, and the dark days of cancer and dying lie ahead.

Tragedy has its way of bringing clarity, doesn't it? The hamster wheel of day in and day out life seems so shallow in the depth of such a loss. The contrast of the darkness of diagnosis and death exposed possibility and even necessity of change for me. I could not ignore the bell that was now ringing louder and louder. Live abundantly. Live fully and completely. Have more fun and do not take it all too seriously. Do not take time for granted. There is no certainty of the gift of tomorrow.

So, the morning of January 1st, I became certain that we would move to the ranch. I could not wait for Wade to rise that day and deliver my big news to him and was confident it would make him so happy.

When we first married, I had set the expectation I would never move to the country and the land his family had built and ranched for generations. So, naturally, he was highly skeptical of my new insight and enthusiasm. On the four-hour car ride back to San Antonio, I kept detailing all the reasons we would move and why it made perfect sense now.

I had set the plans in motion and set a target date of March 15th for the house to be ready for sale. He was on board despite probably doubting the fruition of the plan deep down. He and our dog, Jack, went ahead of me as I prepped the house and closed out our city chapter. The tug of wanting more from our life had won, and we were making our move.

The only uncertainty surfaced when COVID-19 came into light in its big, ugly way. I recall everyone saying how fascinating it was that we had made such a drastic change ahead of such an unforeseeable weird worldwide pandemic. And it made shifts in the business world that made my coaching transition easier. I could shift and adapt with everyone else to zoom meetings and not miss a beat. This brave beginning was working out beautifully. We were finding freedom and discovering amazing satisfaction from simplicity.

Another life learning had surfaced- Never say Never! This move I claimed I would never make was paving the way for great positivity and peace. The inner turmoil, competitive and combative internal dialog had gone to sleep. And I was now sleeping through the night fully and completely as I had never experienced.

My new adventure was giving space to hobbies I had long wanted to pursue with more time and attention, specifically gardening. I had become a Master Gardener in San Antonio and now had the acreage to have the garden of my dreams and I was building it. My mom and dad often ask, "how many sweet potatoes, tomatoes, or onion plants can two people need?" And to that I say, there is always a new variety to try in search of the best one.... it's just fun to grow stuff.

The joy of watching a seed turn into a plant and then produce food is just magical and wondrous to me. And the glowing sunshine warms me through to my soul fully and completely. Living in plenty and possibility fosters more to look toward, too.

I now have what I call white space time to imagine what it might be like to grow for the farmers' market. Or maybe teach gardening to the little folks of the future. Anything is possible and now I am contemplating it and that is exciting. We are only limited by our thoughts, and we get to choose those, at least the second thought anyway, right?

So, an NLP phrase I love is "For what purpose?" I asked that initially about my life, career, and existence. And for me I say… for the Journey of JOY! In pursuing personal growth, I am continually finding fulfillment and meaning. That reward is so promising that it begets the next thing for me.

I surprise myself with the variety of new experiences which lead to new learnings and new conversations, all fostering discovery and curiosity. I can also thank Pinky for the life lesson he gave to me and to remember one of my favorite memories of him in those last days of his heightened sickness.

A different trip to the ranch where we were all outside enjoying a glorious sunny and windy day. He grabbed the kites that were in the utility room and unraveled them and said, lets fly kites enthusiastically. I thought sure!

Grabbing one, I walked out into the field and could not get it to take flight. In his much-weakened state, he made the trek out to me and gave me all the pointers and help I needed to let out the line and let it fly. I will always remember his enthusiasm and spirit of ensuring we all have FUN! Everyone's journey makes impact and matters. Pinky's life and spirit matters still, and I am grateful to have known him.

I now think back to the early days of walking in Mud Creek Park and having a thought "Tiny Matters". I had created a beautiful butterfly garden and was nurturing the Monarchs specifically for their flight to and from Mexico via the I35 corridor through San Antonio called the Monarch Highway. And I saw firsthand how the impact of sowing milkweed seed for the Monarchs in my back yard mattered to the butterflies it fed, sheltered, and created.

I BELIEVE that the combined impact of tiny changes matter. The uniqueness of an individual matters- there is only one YOU. And that makes a difference.

I love the metaphor of the Butterfly Effect, and who knows what is truly possible from the flap of those wings? My purpose is to plant a seed with you today to be and love you. Grow your World. You Matter. Cast your ripple in your special way and feel the fulfillment of knowing that it matters.

"What lies behind us and what lies ahead of us are tiny matters compared to what lies within us." -by Henry Stanley Haskins in 'Meditations in Wall Street'

About Kari K. Whitaker, NLPMP, MTT, MHt, MSC, EFT

 Kari Kelly Whitaker is an Executive Business Coach with Voice of Won. She brings four years of professional experience to her coaching role, having graduated with a Bachelor of Arts in Fashion Merchandising from Southwest Texas State University, Licensed Texas Realtor, as well as holding certifications as Master Practitioner of Neuro-Linguistic Programming, Master Practitioner TIME Techniques, Master Hypnotherapist, Master Life and Success Coach, and EFT Practitioner.

Kari is passionate about helping Realtors, Mortgage Lenders, Title Representatives, and Coaches make more money in less time, creating a life by design rather than default. Her 19 years of experience as a Realtor have earned her a Platinum Top 50 Finalist nominee multiple times, and she is also a Certified Residential Specialist and a Graduate Realtor Institute and Residential Finance Consultant.

Kari as a creative problem solver dedicated to helping her clients reach their goals and is always looking for ways to help them achieve success. Her enthusiasm and passion for her work are evident in everything she does.

To get Kari's gift: THE TOOL to Achieve Any Result in 5 Easy Steps, visit:
www.BPABook.com/gift/Kari

End Every Addiction

Dr. Jeffrey J. Rodman, LPC, LSATP, CCMHt

Below, I summarize my upcoming book, 'End Every Addiction', to be released in mid-2023.

When you think of addiction, you usually think of a hopeless alcoholic or a drug addled heroin addict.

Yet the Merriam-Webster Dictionary defines addiction as "a compulsive, chronic, physiological or psychological need for a habit-forming substance, behavior, or activity having harmful physical, psychological, or social effects and typically causing well-defined symptoms (such as anxiety, irritability, tremors, or nausea) upon withdrawal or abstinence."

You can become addicted to a wide variety of substances, things, behaviors, individuals, and even thought patterns.

While working towards *Becoming Positively Awesome*, it will be critical to *End Every Addiction*, to remove addiction from your mind and body, not just switch to less harmful addictions, less offensive addictions, or to more socially acceptable addictions.

Substance addictions, process addictions, people addictions, thought addictions, and emotional addictions all control your life in such a way as to prevent you from becoming self-actualized, your true self, and meeting the full potential of which you are endowed. You must eliminate addiction from your system so that this burden no longer stands as a barrier between your current self and the new self you are becoming.

Through my Personal Transformation Therapy, you will shed off the old self that is stuck in destructive thinking, feeling, and behavior patterns to create a new identity that supports a healthy self-concept aligned with health, success, prosperity, and freedom.

Basics of Ending Any Addiction

You should never have to go through the pain and suffering that addiction brings. Fortunately, it is possible to end an addiction with the right plan and dedication. But before you can make any real progress in ending your addiction, there are four critical prerequisites:

1. Believe It's Possible: One of the most important steps toward ending every addiction is believing that it's possible to do so. If you don't believe that it can be done, then motivation wanes and it will be difficult for you to really focus on achieving recovery. For recovery to have a fighting chance, you must have a positive mindset and determination, believing that addiction can be overcome.

2. Believe You Can Do It: Not only do you need to believe that ending every addiction is possible, but you also need to believe that it is possible for *you* specifically. This requires faith in yourself and your ability to recover and stay recovered once you have removed addiction from your mind and body. Often,

it's easy to believe other people can end their addiction, but you may believe less in yourself. Maybe you just can't imagine yourself addiction free. Maybe you feel you are too far gone, a lost cause, entangled and hopelessly addicted until the day you die. You may even think addiction is your destiny. This can be very difficult if feelings of self-doubt creep in, which is why it is vitally important to have a comprehensive mind-body based approach, as well as strong support from people who care about you, to overcome an addiction.

3. Decide: Once you believe change is possible, and that change is possible for you, you then need to decide that you want this for yourself. No one else can decide for you - only you have this power within yourself. So, once you understand what is necessary for successful recovery, you must make a firm decision to commit completely towards getting clean and staying clean, no matter what obstacles may arise along the way. And once this decision is made, you must stick by it with every ounce of strength you possess.

4. Believe Someone Else Believes in YOU: You may find it to be too hard, nearly impossible, to believe that this monumental change is possible for you. I get it... in fact, I have been there. If you end up in this desperate position... find someone who you believe in and who believes in you more than you believe in yourself. Someone who believes in you and your ability to

change. Maybe they remember you before your addiction and still see a glimmer of that person shining through. Maybe they have ended their own addiction against impossible odds. Or maybe they just know how easy change can be when you have the right mindset, possess the right tools, and know that anyone can *End Every Addiction* easily and permanently.

I want you to know that, even though I do not know you, I believe in you and your ability to end your addiction completely and permanently. You can do it and I am going to tell you how, what tools to use, how to talk to your doctor, and where to find the help and support you need. I have worked with THOUSANDS of people over the past 20+ years who felt they were hopelessly and permanently addicted who are now living life addiction free.

Thirty-plus years ago, I was "hopelessly and permanently addicted." Almost every male I had ever known was addicted to drugs, alcohol, or both, and most also struggled with a variety of other addictions, such as gambling, codependency, violence, pornography, and more. I started my substance use by age 5, accelerated my use by age 12, and was hopelessly addicted by age 15. By then, I had already dropped out of school and fully expected that I would be dead before my 21st birthday. Obviously, God had other plans and a significant part of that plan was helping others like you to *End Every Addiction* for yourself.

Overcoming an addiction may seem impossible at first glance - but with the basics firmly established, there's nothing stopping you from achieving a healthy lifestyle free from substance dependence!

The Radical Cause Concept: Taking Responsibility for Your Life

Have you ever felt like a victim of your circumstances? Blaming others for your problems and feeling powerless about changing them? It's a common experience, but there's a different way of approaching life that can change everything. The Radical Cause Concept is about choosing to see yourself as being at cause for everything in your life rather than living at the effect of other people.

This doesn't mean that everything is your fault or that you're responsible for other people's actions. It simply means taking full responsibility for your thoughts, feelings, and actions and not allowing others to have control over your identity. By doing so, you become empowered to create the life you want.

When you live at the effect of others, you give away your power. You allow external circumstances and other's actions to determine how you feel and what you do. This can lead to feelings of frustration, helplessness, and resentment. But when you choose to take responsibility for your life, everything changes.

Rather than being a victim, you become the creator of your reality. You see opportunities where before there were only obstacles. Rather than waiting for someone else to make it happen, you take action to create the life you want.

The Radical Cause Concept also means recognizing that everyone has their own journey and their own challenges. It's not about blaming others or judging them for their actions. Instead, it's about acknowledging that we all have our own struggles and that you can only control yourself.

The Radical Cause Concept mindset can be a powerful tool for personal growth and transformation and can help you end every addiction. Addiction is a complex issue that requires support and an effective strategy, and the Radical Cause Concept can be a powerfully helpful tool.

The Radical Cause Concept can be helpful in addressing addictive behaviors by taking responsibility for your thoughts, feelings, and actions related to addiction. Then you can identify the underlying causes of your addiction and take steps toward healing.

For example, instead of blaming external factors or other people for your addiction, you can acknowledge that you have control over your choices and take ownership of your recovery journey. You can also recognize patterns of behavior or thought processes that contribute to the addiction and work towards changing them.

The Radical Cause Concept may not provide a cure-all solution for addiction, but it can be a valuable tool in promoting self-awareness and empowering you to take control of your life.

The Radical Cause Concept is a powerful mindset shift that can transform every aspect of your life. By choosing to see yourself as being at cause for everything in your life, you become an empowered creator rather than a victim of circumstance.

Understanding the Neurological Levels of the Mind

The Neurological Levels of the Mind are an interconnected set of levels from the highest level of your greater self, down to your environment. Each level affects the levels above and below it, and each level can be changed to affect the other levels. The logical levels of the mind are a change model and provide a useful model to understand ways you can achieve change at an individual and organizational level.

The logical levels are: The Greater Self, Identity, Belief, Values, Potential, Behavior, Outcomes, and Environment. Being conscious of the logical levels can help you understand at what level you are attempting to make change.

Sometimes, you might waste time trying to make change at a lower level when you need to consider a higher hierarchical level to achieve that change. If you want to achieve a desired change in life, think about the logical level you are operating.

Be aware of limiting beliefs and the values that feed those beliefs to change the self. Moreso, you must understand the great and unlimited potential within and around you so you can create a new reality.

Shifting Thinking Using Psycho-Cybernetics

The idea of being trapped in an unhealthy cycle is daunting and hard to break free from. Psycho-Cybernetics can help shift your thinking so that you can *End Every Addiction.*

Psycho-Cybernetics is a holistic system for self-improvement that draws from Psychology and Cybernetics - the science of control and communication. This philosophy believes your mind is like a supercomputer, constantly taking in information, processing it, and forming beliefs about yourself. This results in programming that starts at conception, and may even occur generationally, and continues throughout your lifespan. However, if at any point you decide you dislike the outcomes of that programming, you can 'reprogram' your brain to make better decisions and move toward your goals.

You're drawn towards certain things because they bring you comfort or pleasure, but those same things might be unhealthy in certain cases. By recognizing this dynamic, you can start making more conscious choices rather than giving in to impulses that ruin your well-being in the long run.

If you struggle with various addictions, you may belittle yourself or give up when faced with challenges; however, through using this system, you can start viewing 'weaknesses' as potential for growth instead of failure points. By regularly practicing visualization techniques such as picturing success and picturing where you want to be one year from now, you can motivate yourself to stay on track despite any obstacles along the way.

Finally, Psycho-Cybernetic principles allow you to recognize patterns within yourself and learn how best to respond when confronted with triggers or situations which encourage unwanted behaviors. Realizing these patterns helps you build healthier habits by allowing you to take control of what you do when faced with cravings and temptations (which may otherwise pull you down).

End Every Addiction

I will release more on this approach mid-2023, including understanding your mind, types of addictions, detoxing easily, changing your mindset, managing emotions, therapeutic interventions, and relapse prevention.

As a gift for your purchase, please visit my website to download a FREE Journal Workbook to helping you through your journey to End Every Addiction:

www.here-4-you.com/end-every-addiction.html

About Dr. Jeffrey J. Rodman, LPC, LSATP, CCMHt

 Dr. Jeffrey J. Rodman developed a holistic and integrative approach to end every addiction. His upcoming book *End Every Addiction* (mid-2023) and a free Companion Journal is available at www.endeveryaddiction.com.

Dr. Rodman's approach focuses on people's thinking, feelings, and behaviors while helping clients achieve their highest potential. He emphasizes the goodness of clients and works toward each person's growth and self-actualization by helping clients make changes at the identity level. His Personal Transformation Therapy approach uses Hypnotherapy, NLP Brain Training, Emotional Freedom Techniques (EFT), Eye Movement Integration (EMI) and Brain Health Coaching.

Dr. Jeffrey J. Rodman specializes in helping clients eliminate life controlling issues. Dr. Rodman received his BS in Chemical Dependency Counseling and M. Ed. in Counseling and Development from George Mason University, in Fairfax, Virginia, and his PhD in Religion from Christian Bible College in Rocky Mount, NC. He is a Licensed Professional Counselor (LPC), Licensed Substance Abuse Treatment Practitioner (LSATP) in Virginia, and an internationally Board-Certified Clinical Master Hypnotherapist (CCMHt). He holds many additional credentials and certifications and ended his own addiction over 30 years ago.

Adopting an Abundance Mindset for Business and Personal Growth

Jerry Barnett, MSC, MNLP, MTT, MHt

Have you ever had a day where everything seemed to go wrong? No matter how hard you try, you feel you have Charlie Brown's luck. On the other hand, I'm sure you've had days where everything goes right, and you seem to have the Midas touch. Wouldn't it be great if you could have more days like that? Adopting an abundance mindset can do just that, and I have some tips that help me have more of those great days.

You may have heard the saying, "You're never fully dressed until you put on a smile." Not only do you smile because you're in a good mood, the simple act of smiling itself can put you in a good mood. And I'm not talking about putting on a fake smile. Think about something that makes you smile. It's hard to think about something without it affecting your mood.

The law of attraction states that your thoughts dictate your feelings, and your feelings drive your actions, which create your results and shape your world. Since it all starts with your thoughts, why not focus on what you really want?

Have you noticed that successful people are usually pretty positive and optimistic, while people who are down on their luck love to tell you how bad off they have it? What if their

51

outlook on life was not the effect of their circumstances, but the cause of them?

Many people live in effect of their circumstances and have many excuses for their situation in life. They don't realize that taking control of their life is a choice. You may have heard this saying: "There are three types of people: those who make things happen, those who watch things happen, and those who wonder what happened." You can choose to be in that first group and take control of your life rather than simply going along with what life throws at you.

Whenever something doesn't go well for me, I ask myself, "How am I responsible for this? What could I have done to make this situation better? What can I do better next time?" That is a much more empowering mindset than simply throwing my hands in the air and thinking, "Oh, well, it is what it is," and living powerlessly in the effect of my situation. You can choose to take control of the steering wheel and create the life you want.

Keeping a positive mindset is not always easy. Sometimes bad things happen, and you can't seem to stop dwelling on that negativity. Logically, you know that what happens next is not destined to be bad, but you sometimes can't help feeling like that is the case. It takes realizing that you are simply reacting to that situation. Then you can choose to intervene and focus on thinking more positively.

When you find yourself in this situation, there are many things you can do, such as taking a deep, cleansing breath to get centered, focusing on gratitude, or practicing generosity. I don't believe it is coincidence that many of the happiest and most successful people take time from their busy day to meditate, focus on gratitude, and give their time and/or money to help others.

You can also train your brain to automatically seek positivity with this simple and effective mental exercise:

Think about any bad things that happened to you in the past 24 hours. For each one, make a visual representation of that event. If it is a movie, freeze it to a single picture, make it black and white, and shrink that picture down to the size of a postage stamp. Then mentally crumple it up and toss it in the trash in the corner or explode it like fireworks.

Then, think of every good thing that has happened. For each event, replay a short movie clip of it in your mind, seeing, hearing, and feeling the best moment of the event. Then make the movie larger than life and in bright vibrant color. Immerse yourself in how great that experience felt. Turn up that feeling like you turn up the volume on your radio and allow yourself to take a moment and really enjoy that feeling.

Practicing this before bed for a few weeks will train your brain to automatically diminish negativity and focus on positivity.

An abundance mindset can help to find mutually beneficial situations for all parties involved by offering the maximum value in every opportunity.

Another way to think with an abundance mindset is to always look to provide the most value and make every situation mutually beneficial for everyone involved. Whenever you provide more value, you will benefit more. The great thing is, so will everyone else!

I regularly run into people who are always seeking the upper hand. That type of thinking may seem beneficial in the short-term, but it rarely works in the long-term. Even if you get the upper hand, how is the other person going to feel after the dust settles? They may end up feeling taken advantage of and not hold up their end of the deal as whole-heartedly as if they felt you treated them fairly. It could even end up tarnishing your reputation. In the end, if it isn't truly a win-win, it simply won't work out well. People who keep trying to gain the advantage gain no trust, and in my opinion, trust is worth more than a bigger immediate return.

Business dealings do not have to be a zero-sum game. Negotiating a win-win means no one needs to concede anything. It is simply about making sure you are bringing more value to the table so that everyone gets what they want. Think about what you would want if you were in their position. Sometimes things that seem insignificant and easy for you to do can be game changers for them. If it adds value, why not throw it in?

Don't just hope abundance will come to you; program your subconscious to get it for you. Before every meeting, visualize the outcome that you want unfolding just the way you want. Imagine at the end that everyone is smiling, excited, and thanking you for the opportunity as they shake your hand. Then, when you are at the meeting, consider that the person you're meeting is the most important and interesting person you've ever met—and treat them that way. This will help align your mindset and physiology and help prepare you for collaborating with them to find a mutually beneficial solution.

Some people think they need to hoard their value, like it is something that they spend and can run out of. When you give value to someone, you don't lose any, and you don't become less valuable—the value just multiplies. You actually become *more* valuable to them, yourself, and even your future dealings. When you think about value like that, you can't help but feel the abundance!

Here is a good example of this phenomenon in practice. In my web development business, my team and I regularly do minor updates to my client's websites without even being asked to, because I know it will help their business and help them get more clients. After all, the more successful and happier my clients are, the better my reputation becomes as the one who helps small businesses flourish. With over 90% of my business coming from referrals, it is clear that going the extra mile for our clients is much appreciated.

My old scarcity mindset used to be a limiting factor in my decisions, which ended up being a self-fulfilling prophecy. That limited my thinking, which created feelings of scarcity, and held me back from making any decisions that could lead towards progress.

Now, when faced with a decision, I always try to find the option that will increase my future possibilities the most. Often when I'm trying to decide between two things, such as the steak or the shrimp, I ask myself, "Why not both?" Either/or thinking limits your outcome. Both/and thinking is more empowering and expands possibilities. When your brain thinks in terms of abundance, you'll be amazed at the possibilities that you may have not even realized existed.

We all have two sides of us. One side is the best of who you are, which includes your strengths, character, core values, love, kindness. The opposite side is the worst, which has your fears, doubts, needy ego, etc. When you decide from the best side of yourself, you can evaluate the decision based on your values and who you want to become rather than your fears.

When I acted from a scarcity mentality, I was timid and uncertain in my decision making, which often ended up keeping me from deciding at all. As a wise Neal Peart wrote in one of my favorite songs, "If you choose not to decide, you still have made a choice." Without even realizing it, not deciding is really declining the new possibilities and deciding to stay exactly where you are, and that decision is usually made of fear. I've learned that in order to get what I want, I must engage the best side of myself and make the decision that I really want.

Now that I've taken this to heart, decisions are much easier for me. I can weigh the pros and cons more clearly. I like to ask myself if I am more likely to say that I wish I hadn't or I'm glad I did. When I'm 80 years old, will I regret not doing/trying this?

When Jeff Bezos was deciding whether to leave his high-paying job to start Amazon, he thought, "I knew that if I failed, I wouldn't regret that, but I knew the one thing I might regret is not trying." If you made your decisions with that mindset, what would you have done differently and how would your life be different now?

How well do you think you have been making decisions so far? Are you where you thought you would be in life? If so, great, keep it up! If not, it's never too late to make more decisions from an abundance frame of mind now.

Having an abundance mindset is one of the key factors in the success of my business. I used to see any other company who was even close to being in my field as my competition, and therefore my opponent. Once I adopted a mindset of abundance and win-win ideas, I found ways to collaborate with them. Now, some of my most trusted strategic partners are those that I once would avoid.

With my old scarcity mindset, I used to not invest in my business for fear of failing. My old fears and limiting beliefs about my success were holding back business growth. I was scared to invest any more money in my business than I knew I could easily afford, based on my current income. Although that seemed logical, it was the completely wrong way to look at it. Thinking about lack and negativity is no way to expect growth and prosperity.

It wasn't until I adopted these principles and switched my thinking to abundance that business really took off. I've learned that the only real way to grow my business is running and investing in it like I *want it to be* instead of how it currently is. Now, instead of pinching pennies to advertise and make investments in my business, I understand that the more I invest, the more return I get—and many times over.

Another effect of my old way of thinking was that it caused me to question how valuable my company's services were to the marketplace. Since building effective websites came easily to me, I thought there was no way that it was a truly valuable service. I failed to realize that it was the many years of skill-building experience that made it so easy for me and my company to help my clients.

It took a business coach to tell me how rare and valuable my skill set is. My clients can choose to spend years learning those skills or simply pay me to get the same results, and the benefit to their business is worth big bucks to them. It was at that moment that I realized just how valuable my service was to my clients. Since then, I have been more confident that I am bringing much more value than the price I am asking, and that confidence has helped me get even more clients.

If you own a business, are your products and services valuable to others? Of course, otherwise you wouldn't be doing it. It is your duty to let people know so that you can help as many people as you can. How could it possibly be appropriate to limit yourself to helping only a few people when there are so many others that need what you offer?

If you have the skills and ability to help more clients, you will do the universe a great disservice by not doing so. Don't be shy, get out there and tell the world! If you don't promote yourself, nobody else will. If you are not sure how, get the help of a mentor or a trusted advisor to tell your story. Don't wait till the timing is perfect because it will never seem to be perfect. The time to start is now. If you keep doing what you've always done, you'll keep getting what you've always gotten.

As simple as it sounds, adopting an abundance mindset is one of the most effective things you can do to increase your mood, outlook, and success. When used with other positivity techniques, it can easily multiply your results. You will be amazed at the number of mutually beneficial situations presented to you, how easy it is to make decisions that move the needle, and the amount of abundance that seems to find you.

About Jerry Barnett, MSC, MNLP, MTT, MHt

 Board Certified Master Business & Success Coach, Neuro Linguistic Programming Master Practitioner, Master Hypnotist

Jerry Barnett is the founder and CEO of NetShapers (www.netshapers.com), a web development firm in Baton Rouge that specializes in website design, custom software development, and digital advertising. Since 1998, NetShapers has helped businesses of all sizes increase their profits and serve more clients.

After becoming a Certified Networker with the Referral Institute, Jerry became an ambassador for the organization Business Networking International and served as President and mentor of his local chapter.

Most of Jerry's hobbies, such as woodworking and playing various musical instruments, involve creating things that are both esthetic and functional. He also fulfills that passion when designing innovative ways to help businesses reach their goals and is personally involved with every project. Jerry strives to forge long-term relationships with his clients, and his drive comes from helping others succeed.

He attributes his success to being a lifelong learner and finding creative solutions to new challenges.

To get Jerry's gift, visit:
www.BPABook.com/gift/Jerry

Harnessing the Power of Affirmations and Visualizations for Self-Actualization

Aloha J. McGregor, LPC, NCC, MNLP, MTT, MHt

As a mental health professional, I know all too well the importance of focus. The conversations we have with ourselves and the way we choose to envision ourselves now and, in the future, play a vital role in how we live out our lives.

We are biologically and psychologically created to interact with our environment in a way that is aligned with our focus. The troubling thing is that we focus on the part of our lives that does not line up to what is really important to us. We are created to live or die by the way we think and speak.

This chapter is not meant to be in the spiritual context but as a spiritual being I would be remiss if I did not point out that we are physically made, told to speak a certain way, and to think on specific things. Doing so leads to our being able to live victorious, peaceful lives, as is promised.

Whether we speak and think positive or negative, we create our reality. Our biological and physiological selves will work the way they are designed to work.

After the initial assessment with every client I counsel, the very first thing I do is discuss this. Fully understanding that for most of them, positive thoughts, talk, or perspective are never immediate. The automatic side is almost always the negative until we have made an intentional effort not to be.

My saying to them is "Be intentional until it's habitual." Do it on purpose until it becomes natural. It will make it easier when we must. So now I am going to share with you what I share with all.

Affirmations and Visualizations: How They Work and Their Benefits

Affirmations are positive statements that influence the subconscious mind, which control our beliefs, attitudes, and behaviors. By consciously choosing a short, specific, present-tense, positive, and personal statement and repeating it frequently throughout the day, we can reinforce the positive belief and strengthen its impact on the subconscious mind.

There are different affirmations, including self-affirmations, interpersonal affirmations, goal-oriented affirmations, and guided affirmations. These can help promote self-confidence, healthy relationships, motivation, and relaxation. The key to making affirmations work is to believe in the statement being repeated and to practice them consistently.

The power of positive affirmations lies in their ability to shift our mindset and beliefs from negative to positive, helping us break free from limiting beliefs and self-talk that hold us back and replace them with empowering thoughts and beliefs. Affirmations serve as an inspirational reminder of all that we can achieve, enabling us to define and create what we want in life.

Visualizations, on the other hand, are mental images or pictures of a desired outcome or situation created in the mind's eye through imagination. They work by creating a sensory experience that stimulates the same areas of the brain as a real-life experience, thus creating new neural pathways and strengthening existing ones. Repeatedly visualizing a desired outcome makes the brain accept this image as real and work towards making it a reality, aligning our conscious and unconscious desires and beliefs.

There are different visualizations, including outcome visualization, process visualization, creative visualization, and mental rehearsal, that can help individuals achieve their goals by motivating them, improving their performance, cultivating a positive and empowered mindset, and practicing specific skills or actions.

In summary, affirmations and visualizations are powerful tools that can help individuals promote positive change in their lives, break free from limiting beliefs and self-talk, and create a more positive and empowered mindset. The key to making them work is to believe in the statements and images being repeated and to practice them consistently.

The Synergy of Affirmations, Visualizations, and Self-Actualization

Self-actualization refers to the highest level of psychological development, according to Abraham Maslow's hierarchy of needs. It is the process of becoming the best version of oneself, realizing one's full potential, and achieving personal growth and fulfillment.

Maslow described self-actualization as the desire to become everything that one can become. This includes having a sense of purpose, meaning, and personal identity, as well as a desire for self-fulfillment, creativity, and achievement.

Self-actualized individuals have a strong sense of morality, creativity, and authenticity. They are driven by personal growth and development, rather than external rewards or recognition. They can also accept themselves and others for who they are and have a deep sense of connection to the world around them.

Self-actualization is an achievable goal for anyone willing to put in the effort, and affirmations and visualizations can be powerful tools to help attain it. When used together, affirmations and visualizations can create a synergistic effect that reinforces positive beliefs and attitudes, helping individuals to develop a sense of inner confidence and motivation that can lead to the achievement of their goals.

For instance, someone seeking to improve their public speaking skills may use affirmations like "I am confident and articulate when I speak" and combine them with visualization techniques, like mentally rehearsing a successful speech. This can help create a sense of inner confidence and motivation, leading to increased confidence and preparedness during an actual speech.

To use affirmations and visualizations together, follow these steps:

1. Identify a specific goal or outcome that you want to achieve, such as in your career, relationships, health, or personal development.
2. Create a positive affirmation that directly relates to your goal. Your affirmation should be a positive statement that reflects the outcome you desire and should be in the present-tense. For example, "I am happy and fulfilled in my career."

   Adding emotional triggers into the affirmations can increase their power and effectiveness. For example, if your goal is to become more confident in social situations, instead of affirming "I am becoming increasingly confident", adding the words "I feel calm and relaxed when talking to people" will help create an emotional connection between the affirmation and its desired outcome.
3. Use your affirmation as a basis for your visualization. Create a mental image of yourself experiencing the outcome you desire and incorporate your affirmation into this image. For example, visualize yourself in a job you love, surrounded by supportive colleagues, and making a meaningful impact. Repeat your affirmation as you visualize and focus on the positive emotions associated with achieving your goal. Use all

your senses to make the visualization vivid and detailed.

4. Use your affirmation and visualization consistently, ideally daily. Repeat your affirmation regularly throughout the day and take time each day to visualize your desired outcome. Repeated use of affirmations will cement their message into your subconscious, allowing you to stay focused on achieving the desired outcome while also bringing joy and positivity into your day.

How Affirmations and Visualizations Work

By combining affirmations and visualizations, individuals can achieve self-actualization by developing a positive mindset and creating a sense of inner confidence and motivation. These tools can help individuals stay focused on their goals, leading to greater success and fulfillment in all areas of life.

Affirmations and visualization techniques have the power to change our internal dialog and beliefs, which can create a roadmap towards self-actualization. These tools interact with the Reticular Activating System (RAS) to help filter out distractions and prioritize information that reinforces our beliefs and goals.

The RAS acts as a filter for the brain, allowing only the most important stimuli to reach our conscious awareness. By directing our attention towards positive beliefs and outcomes, we can signal the RAS that these things are important. This can lead to a shift in behavior, an increase in motivation, and a heightened awareness of opportunities and resources that can help us achieve our goals.

Ultimately, this process can lead to a positive transformation of our thoughts, beliefs, and behaviors, creating lasting changes in our lives. To make the most of the affirmations and visualization, it's important to identify a specific goal or outcome, create a positive affirmation, visualize the desired outcome, and repeat these practices consistently. By doing so, we can create an internal GPS towards self-actualization, helping us stay focused, motivated, and aligned with our goals.

Whether your intention is self-actualization in the broad sense of the word, to actualize any other step in the hierarchy of needs, to improve wellbeing, or to meet long or short goals, the process is the same.

Remember, you were created biologically and psychologically with systems (nervous system, RAS, conscious and subconscious, and Spirit) in place for you to create the life you want. And if you are a believer, to have peace, joy, and to have the life you are promised. The instruction book tells us to think on things that are true, honest, just, pure, lovely, of good report, virtuous, and praiseworthy (Philippians 4:8) and to choose life by speaking life.

Affirm yourself, affirm yourself in God, speak the promises of God, or declare biblical truths, and create visualization to

67

set your internal GPS. Just like when you do so in your car, set it and forget; the navigation system does what it is programmed to do.

Also, like getting behind the wheel, you must do the work of driving the car, paying attention to the road, and listening to the signals given by the system. All your systems are guiding you, but you must do the work.

If you get off track, you will be rerouted. If there are roadblocks, you will be provided a detour. Follow the rules of the road and you will get to your destination. Remember, you have a choice; there are alternate routes, so choose the fastest, the one without tolls, or the scenic one. Setting the GPS is the first step.

About Aloha J. McGregor, LPC, NCC, MNLP, MTT, MHt

 Aloha J McGregor is a Licensed Professional Counselor (LPC). She has a Master of Arts degree in Clinical Mental Health Counseling and a bachelor's degree in Christian Counseling from Liberty University.

She has also earned professional certification from the National Board for Certified Counselors and works as a National Certified Counselor (NCC). Along with her education as a counselor, she is also a licensed Minister. Aloha is a board certified as a Master clinical hypnotherapist and Master Neuro-linguistic programming (NLP), TIME Technique, and EFT practitioner.

Her other noteworthy accreditations include being a member of the Psi Chi National Honor Society, a member of the American Association of Christian Counselors, International Board of Coaches and Practitioners (IBCP) and being part of the Licensed Professional Counselors Association of Georgia.

Aloha started her private practice Mending Minds Counseling and Coaching Group in 2020. To find out more about services and products visit www.mendingmindscounselinggroup.com

For your free gift:
www.BPABook.com/gift/Aloha

"The way to happiness: Keep your heart free from hate, your mind from worry. Live simply, expect little, give much. Fill your life with love. Scatter sunshine. Forget self; think of others. Do as you would be done by. Try this for a week, and you will be surprised."

Norman Vincent Peale

Dare to be True

Kiersten Blest, CCHt, NLPP, PTT, CSC, EFT

Most people have a story they don't tell out loud, one they keep buried and locked inside. Maybe it's from their childhood, a more recent time, or maybe it's still unfolding.

It's the story that makes them feel alone, no matter how many people surround them. They feel no one understands exactly what they feel or why and that no one really knows them.

There's a voice inside their head that makes them feel they're never enough. And no matter what they do or how hard they try, they can't shake feeling bad about themselves. And no one knows how they spin in self-doubt or how they worry other people will criticize or judge them.

I don't know their story, but I know their fears. And it becomes an exhausting way to live.

* * *

"I need another part."

That's my opening line, how I plan to start the conversation with Ron. Not a conversation, really, more like a demand disguised as a cordial request with an undertone of required respect. I pray for a quick exchange. My emotions teeter between desperate and furious, which, even at fifteen, I know results in defeat. I need to find the perfect

71

combination of indifferent and firm, so the conversation is swift and my problem of the day rapidly disappears.

His studio mirrors a dungeon, especially at this time of day, concealed in the depths of the Academy. There's nothing to do while I wait for Ron except breathe in his stale cigarette smoke and the spine-chilling secrets trapped in the air that no one is ready to catch and reveal.

Forcing my teeth to unclench, I flick on the lights and silently instruct my face to behave.

My face is permanently labeled as a problem by both my parents and teachers. Whether I'm gazing off into a vast space of nothingness, rolling my eyes, scrunching my eyebrows, or glaring at someone, there's no miscalculating what I'm thinking.

But the worst is when someone launches bullets of spiteful words directly into my heart because the corners of my mouth plunge to the base of my chin, releasing a flood of salted water all over my face. The faucet opens less frequently now, but only because I've built a massive dam that holds barrels of tears in reserve.

The dam protects me from my father. Tears of any kind make his academically brilliant head burst. The consequences of crying are as severe as talking back and not paying attention. Those consequences multiply exponentially when other people are around because my parents are obsessed with what other people think.

So, it mattered in kindergarten when I was displayed on the Academy's pink bench for clunking a boy with my lunchbox because I thought he was cute. It mattered when my first-grade teacher dropped me into a lower reading group for taking too long to flip pages. It mattered when teachers testified at parent-teacher conferences that I didn't pay attention, spent too much time sharpening my pencil, talking to my neighbor, going to the bathroom, or visiting the nurse. And it mattered when I didn't get picked for a part in a play, recital, or receive some award because it all blared like a five-alarm fire that there were parents raising children who outshined me.

That's how my parents saw it.

If they could see me now, pacing back and forth, choking on my opening line, they would tell me to take my sneakers off, stop wearing a hole in the already worn carpet, sit down, be quiet, or go home.

I sit down. Gripping my knees tight into my chest, practicing my line in different pitches and paces, and rocking back and forth, the same as the morning my father punished me for taking his silver pen without asking. The missing pen set him off. My lying made it worse, and the array of crayons and coloring books that landscaped my bedroom floor fueled the already-stoked fire.

I was confined to my room for more days than it took to recover from pneumonia, left with emptied bookshelves and a vacant toy chest, as stuffed animals were re-homed to the trash. It was enough time for the tiny voice in my head to become a constant reminder that I wasn't smart enough, I couldn't throw a ball far enough, I couldn't run fast enough, my piano playing wasn't slow enough, my speaking wasn't clear enough, and my writing wasn't smooth enough. She reminded me of everything I knew about myself by the time I was seven, including the ornaments I made that weren't pretty enough to put on the Christmas tree.

I remember the first ornament, an uneven circle cut from cardboard with cotton fluff for snow, a hand-drawn Christmas tree sprinkled with red glitter, and a tiny gold foil sticker star on top. I flew through the house and burst into the clean bathroom my mother was re-cleaning. "Look what I made!"

She tilted her head from the sink, gave it a once-over, and said it was nice before peeling off her gloves and picking the red glitter off my face with pointy fingernails and a frown.

She went back to scrubbing.

I crept down the stairs to the Christmas tree, pushed a glossy silver bell out of my way, and hung my red glitter tree in its place while the corners of my mouth slightly perked up.

That Christmas Eve, when my grandparents arrived, my red glitter tree was nowhere to be found.

We never discussed that ornament or much else. My parents were in charge as democracy stopped at the front door.

So, they sent me to the Academy, wearing scratchy dresses and a beehive bun, while everyone else dressed and smiled the same. They sent me to ballet lessons because baseball was for boys. They ordered me to say yes, to do what I was told, and eat everything on my plate, even when dinner was served with a diet of rules and criticism that concluded with piercing words, booming voices, and someone's hand slamming on the kitchen table.

Stop wasting food; money doesn't grow on trees; how many times do we need to tell you, try harder, stop being so sensitive, stop crying over spilled milk, toughen up, put a smile on your face, stop causing us problems, why should we bother with you, you don't listen, why can't you be more like Suzy down the street, maybe we should send you away, the world doesn't revolve around you, sit still, be quiet, stop talking, stop crying, I'll give you something to cry about, wipe that look off of your face, or I'll wipe it off for you, it's our way or the highway, as long as you're under this roof, you'll do things our way because we said so, what happens in this house stays in this house, do you understand?

It was an unforgiving, unrelenting family diatribe passed down from generation to generation on both sides of my DNA chain, which I couldn't escape and never asked for.

I almost escaped the Academy, but I was too afraid people would think I got kicked out. Instead, I spent eight months with a teacher who scolded me for asking questions, insisted I didn't try hard enough, regularly reported to my parents that I refused to ask for help, and reprimanded me for crying almost every morning. My problems at the Academy reached an all-star level when the boy in the black coat made his debut.

He slid in as part of a fresh cluster of students and walked the halls as if he had built them. He was gifted with words and skilled at making you feel warm if things went his way. But he also brought his own pot of emotional soup, which he received the day he lost what mattered most. He tried to keep it covered; some days, he did. And those days together were calm.

But you never knew when someone would turn up the heat, stir the pot the wrong way, or peek into the pot without asking. And you didn't know if the pot would steam, boil, overflow, or blow its cover straight to the ceiling.

I stirred the pot the wrong way and became blackened, burned, and charred to the bone. But burns weren't enough because his blazing tongue, with its razor-sharp blade, was still slicing those scabs back open. And no matter how skilled I've become at dodging and ducking his slashes throughout every hallway; the boy still clips my heels and scrapes my blisters because he hasn't stopped slicing them open yet.

So, there is no way I will be placed next to him on stage and cast in a part that requires me to smile and chit-chat with him.

* * *

It wasn't until I cleared the building that my dam finally collapsed. Ron didn't share many reasons; I gave him a small portion of mine. But his decision to keep me in the same role *"would be good for me"*. Those were his parting words.

Many years later, when the rest of my story unfolded, I understood for the first time that he was right.

People ask how I got from where I was then to where I am now. The conversation with Ron was the first step. He taught me one of the most important life lessons I could learn: the only way to overcome fear is to move *through it*.

I took another small step a few months later, pushing myself through fear. Despite being rejected the prior year, I auditioned again for the Speech Team, something I would never have considered before. I went on to win many tournaments during the rest of my time at the Academy.

But my real inner work began when my son was born. It was time to break the generational parenting patterns I experienced as a child. It was time to change who I was and become the person I wanted to be.

I freed myself from old negative thinking patterns through the powerful gift of NLP. I learned that we each have a lens through which we see the world, and our personal experiences, values, and beliefs define that lens. This explains how two people can take part in the same event yet experience it differently. Mastering this concept removed overwhelming pressure and stress. When I realized I can't control how others see or experience me, I stopped taking criticism personally and worrying about what others think.

It also opened the door to forgiveness and reconciliation with the past. I saw everyone in a new light, including my parents. When we meet people, we don't know what they've been through or why they see the world the way they do. It opens us up to compassion, creating space so we listen to everyone we meet with two ears instead of one.

I learned the hard way the importance of releasing emotional pain quickly. Holding on to negative feelings for too long destroys emotional and physical health. The challenge is that many people don't realize they have unresolved emotions because they're buried so deep that they don't discover them until their body responds.

My unresolved emotions expressed themselves through panic attacks and agoraphobia, paralyzing me from fully living for years. Many people hold on to emotions because they don't want to surface old memories, but there are several effective and gentle techniques, including guided EFT and Hypnotherapy, that can help release emotions without reliving tough experiences.

I stopped looking to the outside world for approval which was one of the more challenging lessons I learned. We move through family, school, and work systems that reward us for reaching milestones, achievements, and status from the moment we walk to the moment we retire. And while we enjoy the recognition and feel-good feelings when we achieve certain success and status, these systems provide a dangerous and distressing emotional trap.

* * *

If one believes they have a soul purpose, discovering it through Human Design is a tremendous gift. It brings to their awareness what they came here to learn and do, who they are at their core, and how to navigate life with less resistance. The magic of Human Design is unlocking one's gifts, strengths, inherent value, and undeniable worth in ways that nothing else can explain.

Our Experiences may vary, but we share the same journey of self-discovery, healing, and expansion. There are knots to unwind and webs to untangle, but once that work is done, one we can discover our true purpose and worth. Moving beyond complete self-acceptance to a place of self-love is powerful and unconditional. The life we long to create, filled with peace, positivity, love, and success, no longer exists outside of us; it emerges from within us.

As it emerges, we create a new story.

About Kiersten Blest, CCHt, NLPP, PTT, CSC, EFT

 Kiersten Blest is a Transformation Coach, Clinical Hypnotherapist, and Practitioner of NLP, EFT, Quantum Human Design™, and The Quantum Alignment System™. She has more than 25 years of corporate experience helping established and emerging leaders accelerate their professional success. She is a graduate of Bentley University with a BS in Business Management and is a Six Sigma Green Belt. She is also the founder of My New Life LLC.

Kiersten has worked with hundreds of clients to help them overcome the effects of difficult relationships. Her clients elevate confidence and overcome stress, fears, and overwhelm while freeing themselves from self-defeating thought patterns and lingering emotions. Her expertise in clinical hypnotherapy, NLP, and numerous other science and energy-based modalities, combined with her corporate experience, makes her uniquely qualified to guide her clients through the process of rewriting their narrative and discovering who they are at their core, while paving the path for greater success in their personal and professional lives.

Kiersten believes that our past does not need to define us. She provides her clients with the tools they need to unlock their full potential and create a more empowering, successful, and fulfilling life.

www.KierstenBlest.com

Ancestral DNA:
Adventures Through Time Travel

Lura J. Dahlem, MAPM, MNLP, MCHt, MSC, MTT

Today is a bright new day. It's a day where we can begin to build extraordinary lives with all the joys and delights that we seek. But what if that's *not quite true* for all of us? What if *some of us* are predestined to live our lives as our ancestors have, in not so pleasing ways?

Is it possible that the dreams and cautionary tales we experience in the stories of our families, both real and embellished, could predetermine our own challenges and experiences—and those of future generations? How much of our lives is programmed within us before we're even born, and how much is created (*and passed on*) by the traumas of the lives we live and what we now think?

Could it be that our very DNA is already programmed for loss, pain, and victimhood to sabotage every happiness we seek? Can we change it? And just how do our deep desires come about—the impulses, longings, and yearnings that we follow to build what we *believe* is a life of our own?

I first stumbled upon the concept of ancestral DNA when I was introduced to a study concerning mice and trauma. It was reported that once mice experienced a trauma stimulus, such as an electric shock, they would behave differently upon being placed back into a familiar maze. The most interesting factor was that their offspring, who had not

81

yet been introduced to the maze, displayed the same post-shock stressed behavior upon entering the testing area, even without their own electrical trauma experience.

But then it gets even better! When researchers would resolve the trauma response within the later generations, it also altered the traumatic response of earlier generations without direct interaction by the research team! Healing the grandchildren's generation seemed to allow the grandparents to heal from what had originally happened to them!

Years later, I was introduced to an ancient Greek concept for generational healing that released past familial traumas through prayer and visualization using *ekteinô* (*to reach beyond what is*). Using this concept, when a subject would visualize resolving the root cause of a generational affliction, all generations would experience the relief and recovery from that disease or disorder. Could it really be that simple?

During an excursion to Greece in 2015, I visited the ancient ruins of Delphi, the site where the very first "hospital" was erected in the world. I found not only the ruins of an ancient temple where the first doctors treated injury and disease, and the Oracle of Delphi gave out bits of wisdom, but also a theater where plays were performed with deliberate intent. The ancient Greeks believed that to heal the body, one must also heal the mind. Each hospital was paired with a theater so that any patient who received both care and inspiration could heal fully and completely from whatever ailed them.

As a wellness practitioner, I have sat and listened to thousands of clients over the years as they rehearse the stories from their childhoods and those of their parents and grandparents, explaining the chain of events that led them to their current circumstances. I say "rehearse" deliberately, for it is the stories that we tell ourselves and others that determine the potential outcomes we seek (and find) for ourselves, especially at the *subconscious* level.

I have been trained throughout the years to ignore the content of the story I'm being told, and to listen for the belief system and other subconscious clues that give meaning to what *can and cannot happen* for my client within their own unconscious programming. Sometimes it only takes a simple reframe to open the client's mind to possibilities that will get them to their desires. Other times, it takes much more, but it can almost always be accomplished. And once a thing is possible in the mind, the momentum toward its accomplishment can fully begin.

One of my favorite tools to use with clients who are "stuck" in the concept of what they can or cannot do, is to go back in time to the origin of an emotional event and change the meaning that is attached to that event. Once the meaning changes, the emotions are released, and new possibilities open up immediately. I adjusted this technique, going even further back in time, and "inhabiting" generational ancestors—changing how family stories were being used to justify a client's inability to choose differently. I often heard things like, "In my family, we just don't get ahead." Or

"Since I come from a family who…." And so it went. They believed they were predisposed to the circumstances they were living in, and a change in direction for their own story was not really an option.

One particular client came to me with challenging anxiety and feelings of never being good enough. As we talked about how she represented these beliefs in her mind, she told me stories of Catholic ancestors who had come over from Ireland during the harrowing times of the potato famine. Reaching New York in the 1840s, they found respite in the Irish communities where familiar voices and traditions brought the community together.

Outside of these neighborhoods, however, the Irish were not well looked upon. They were subjected to much discrimination and treated as second-class citizens and outcasts. Poverty was prevalent in their districts. Hard work, perseverance and keeping your head down became a way of survival. Many were indentured servants who owed years of servitude to their masters to repay their fares for a voyage across the sea.

Many Irish immigrants learned to stay hyper-alert and keep watch over their own, always seeing themselves as potential victims for the more prosperous and well-established inhabitants of the city. Was it possible that the ancestral emotions of these immigrants had actually caused an emotional DNA chain reaction to occur that would predispose my client to anxiety and limit her ability to develop a healthy sense of self-worth? I was curious to check it out.

Using an NLP time travel technique and the gift of imagination, together we embarked on a journey back to 1840 Catholic Ireland. Within an imagined experience, my client could recognize within her own body the emotions that such an impoverished and persecuted climate would have invoked in her ancestors. Addressing the emotional feelings and sensations, and the meanings they gave to life in those times, I led her through release techniques, allowing her to recover emotional resources and change the way she perceived her ancestors' lives. We reframed the possibilities from hope-less to hope-full, and then allowed those strengths to be passed on from that generation, forward throughout the ancestral bloodline.

There was an incredible sense of release and understanding that took place for my client—her perspective of both her own life story and the anxiety she carried, and of the self-worth that she had struggled with since childhood shifted. Just being able to tell a new uplifting story about the family immigration saga, and the perceived effect it had on future generations, was priceless for my client's mindset.

So, how does all this work and how can we use it to buoy up our lives for more joy and momentum along our way? To begin, we know that the language of the subconscious mind is the language of imagination. Most prevalently, it is the language of pun, paradox, and metaphor. When we tell the stories of our lives, and of those who came before us, we are painting a picture of just how we find order in the world—where we may tread, and what is forbidden to us.

When we speak, we are often unaware of the limits that our language sets for us. We then flail against some unknown adversary to thrive in life. The truth is, our stories are the only adversary that we really need to overcome in order to prosper. How we phrase the events in our lives ("I'm the kind of person who...") and the mindset with which we set our assumptions -- what will be effortless and what will be difficult for us ("Dad always said us Johnsons were the hardest-working people") -- create the palette from which we paint. And rarely does that default color scheme of victimhood change throughout the years or the generations.

But what about the science of Ancestral DNA, and not just the stories of the mind? Does it have any credibility in the world of experience? We have all heard stories about identical twins who were raised apart from their parents and each other, yet each maintains some character trait, or some skill set (be it music, career, or other interest) that links them back to the biological parents and ancestors within their bloodline.

Is part of our DNA actually remembering *their prior choices and experiences* — the prior loves, hates, traumas and desires of those who came before us? Is that preference or experience now imprinted within the genetic code of our own existence? And what about future generations? Will they continue to create within their lives the same experiences that you and I are creating today?

The work of today's leading researchers and scientists in epigenetics seems to support the belief that *the past is indeed imprinted into our genes.* Dr. Bruce Lipton, Ph.D., shocked the world when his research announced that you can alter your genetics by modifying your behavior. Can the choices we make, and the resulting actions we take, actually alter our genetic code? And does this history affect the generations that come after us?

Let's look at the story of a European soldier who refused to fight in World War I and how his choices seemed to affect the lives of future generations. James was a typical farmer and mechanic in the early 1980s in Iowa. He was working on a piece of farm equipment near his barn when his hand slipped, and the sharp edge of the blade severed his thumb from his right hand. After a successful surgery to reattach his thumb, his father visited him. "You know," the older man told his son, "My father also cut off his right thumb when he was about your age."

Curious, James asked more questions and found that his grandfather, George, after immigrating from his homeland in Europe in the 1940s, suffered an accident while working at a factory in Philadelphia, severing his right thumb.

Several years later, James' daughter was doing genealogical research on her father's family, and found documentation where his great-grandfather, William, had been called up for duty to fight in the Great War of 1917, but instead of complying with his assignment, he used a hunting knife to slice the thumb from his right hand so that he could no longer hold a rifle. William was vilified by his community as a coward, and never really recovered from his choices.

In this instance, the family stories were unknown. So, is it a coincidence that men in the family suffer accidents that maim their right thumbs, or is it an ancestral imprint that follows them through their genetic code? And what, if anything, can they do about it?

In the work I've done with clients throughout the last three decades, I've found that both perspectives can be true: the incredible (and often unknown) events and preferences of past generations can creep into the life experiences of those who are living and working today; AND, the stories that we share about our family, our history, and recurrent ancestral events in the past may also affect our lives and that of future generations. These stories affect the programming that runs our subconscious minds, often creating hazardous patterns for us, of which we are mostly unaware.

I am excited to combine release techniques for the stories we know, and the meanings that our family histories (or even the lack thereof) give to these stories with ancestral genealogy. This can uncover some of the primary patterns of historical experiences in our family lines. When we clear the subconscious mind of the predisposition to *choose only that which is familiar to us* ("I'm the kind of person who...") AND we clear the ancestral patterns of *what it means* to come from a family who hasn't chosen a happy, healthy, wealthy existence for themselves, we can then clear the slate, reframe beliefs about our own existence, and open up to the very good possibility of a life of success and happiness.

In working on the genealogy of my family, I've found parallels in my life that were previously unknown. I have several ancestors who were in law enforcement in the last 200 years. Did their choices influence my decision to work as a deputy jailer and later to marry a probation officer?

With two degrees in theology, I was surprised to find several preachers in my lineage, including Martin Luther (Lutter). And as a college professor, I later learned that both my maternal grandparents had planned to be educators in the 1930s, but never reached their dreams. Are these Ancestral Imprints in my DNA?

In my practice, I have seen how a buried past can repeat itself in new generations and in new ways through the stories my clients tell. Reframing that past can allow them the freedom to choose differently.

But the real question that has yet to be answered is this: *When our feelings change, does our generational future change as well?* This, I find intriguing. Since you cannot change that of which you are unaware, as we become more aware, does everything change? How far forward and how far back? Hmmm.

About Lura J. Dahlem, MAPM, MNLP, MCHt, MSC, MTT

 Lura Dahlem is a professor, master wellness practitioner, success coach, mentor, and proud grandmother to two amazing kids and one grand-dog. She has always been fascinated with the seemingly magical ways people can thrive and prosper in life.

Lura holds three degrees: one in Business and two in Pastoral Ministry. Her background includes roles as a social worker, graduate school registrar, adjunct professor, lay minister, entrepreneur, and founder and CEO of Living ALOT, Inc. with two client offices in Northern Oklahoma.

She has taught a variety of subjects at the graduate school level, such as Emotional Intelligence, Servant Leadership, Ethics, and Organizational Behavior. Lura is also a co-author of the book, Peeling Back the Layers. She has served thousands of client hours, both online and in-person, specializing in releasing emotional trauma and chronic pain.

Lura is board certified through IBCP and IHF as a Master NLP Practitioner, Master Clinical Hypnotherapist, Master Success Coach, and Master Wellness Practitioner. Her passion for her work is evident in the life she has created.

Get Lura's gift at: www.BPAbook.com/gift/Lura

For more information on the work Lura does and the services she provides, please visit her website at https://www.LivingALOT.com

Mindset Movement Manifest

Aruna Ramamurthy B. Sc., LMT, ISSA-CPT, NLPP

Let me share with you a story of this young woman who grows up in a small town with her parents as her role models. She is naturally zestful, bubbly yet nerdy, happy, caring, compassionate, strong, and determined to accomplish the goals she sets for herself, even as a child in high school.

She told her father that she would like her parents to choose the right person for her to marry after she completes her college education and earns a degree. Her parents agree with her.

She gets married to this man 11 days before she turns 22. She starts her journey as his wife, with all the dreams and desires without a clue of what is in store for her.

 This man quickly shows her his true colors within 2 months of marriage with his abusive language, which makes her question her own value for the first time. As days go by, though, she witnesses he would take any measure to please his mom. Even if that means physical, emotional, verbally abusing this young woman in front of his mom and his family to earn his brownie points.

After 1.5 years, she gives birth to a beautiful boy. This young woman still loves her husband authentically, though he hasn't changed a bit. And she endures 3rd degree burns to 45% of her body after a heated argument with him and hospitalized for 27 days while going through skin grafts. She continues in that abusive relationship for another 15 years before she STANDS UP FOR HERSELF AND BECOMES A ROLE MODEL.

Here are the lessons she shares:

Positive Mindset is Key to Success

While it's challenging to hear harsh words from someone close to you, there are ways to use those words to improve yourself and show resilience. Here are some tips:

1. Don't Take it Personally: Remember that the harsh words are likely not a reflection of your true worth, but a reflection of the other person's own feelings and frustrations. Try not to take it personally and instead focus on the message they are trying to convey.

2. Look for Constructive Feedback: Try to identify any constructive feedback within the harsh words. Even if the delivery is not ideal, there may be useful information or suggestions that can help you improve in a specific area.

3. Practice Self-Reflection: Take some time to reflect on the situation and consider if there is any truth to what they said. If there is, use this as an opportunity for personal growth and improvement.

4. Stay Calm and Composed: Instead of reacting emotionally, try to stay calm and composed. This will

show the other person you are not easily shaken and can handle criticism maturely.

5. Respond with Kindness and Respect: Responding with kindness and respect can help to defuse a tense situation and show the other person you will not engage in negativity or hostility. This can also help to foster a more positive dialog.

With the right mindset and approach, you can use these situations to improve yourself and show your strength and resilience.

Take SMALL, CONSISTENT ACTIONS

Remember, starting a big project can be challenging, but by taking small, consistent actions, you can make progress and achieve your goals.

Setting a deadline and consistently working on one like filing taxes or organizing paperwork can help you stay motivated and make steady progress towards your goal.

By breaking the project down into smaller tasks and taking consistent action, you can work towards completing the project by the deadline and free up time to focus on other activities that you enjoy. It's important to stay focused on the end goal and celebrate small successes along the way to maintain momentum and motivation. With a bit of planning, discipline, and determination, you can accomplish these projects, and enjoy the benefits of your hard work by overcoming any initial resistance or fear of getting started.

Celebrate Your Progress

Celebrating your progress is an important part of achieving your goals. It's important to take time to acknowledge your accomplishments and give yourself credit for the hard work you've put in.

Celebrating your progress with yourself first can help to build self-confidence and reinforce positive habits. It can be as simple as taking a moment to reflect on what you've achieved or treating yourself to something special as a reward for your hard work.

Celebrating your progress with like-minded people can also be beneficial. Sharing your successes with others who understand the challenges and joys of working towards a goal can help to build a sense of community and support. It can also inspire others to pursue their own goals and celebrate their progress along the way.

Ultimately, the key is to find a balance between celebrating your progress and staying focused on your goals. Celebrating too much can lead to complacency, while not celebrating enough can lead to burnout and a lack of motivation. By finding a balance and celebrating your progress along the way, you can stay motivated and make steady progress towards achieving your goals.

Discouraging Words: View and Use Them as a Tool

Discouraging words can be challenging to hear, but it's important to use them as a tool for motivation rather than allowing them to hold you back.

By taking action and moving forward towards your goals, you can create momentum in your progress and prove to yourself and others that you can achieve great things.

Movement and creative expression can be powerful tools for building confidence and motivation.

When you are engaged in an activity that you enjoy and that brings you fulfillment, it can help to drown out the discouraging words and keep you focused on your goals.

Whether it's exercise, dance, yoga, jogging, or any other form of creative expression, the movement can help to propel you forward in your journey and give you the energy and motivation you need to keep going.

Ultimately, the key is to stay focused on your goals and use any discouraging words or obstacles as motivation to prove your strength and value. By taking action, you can create momentum in your progress and prove to yourself and others that you can achieve great things.

HEALTHY BOUNDARIES = Tools to MANIFEST

Having healthy boundaries with family and friends is important for several reasons, including the ability to manifest your goals and dreams. When you have healthy boundaries, you can focus on what is important to you without being pulled in too many directions.

Remember, setting healthy boundaries is an important part of taking care of yourself and manifesting your goals. It may feel uncomfortable at first, but by staying true to your priorities and values, you can achieve great things and build strong, supportive relationships with those around you. Here are some ways to practice healthy boundaries:

Protect Your Time and Energy: When you set healthy boundaries, you can protect your time and energy, which is essential for staying focused on your goals. This means saying no to things that don't serve you or align with your priorities.

Stay Focused on Your Goals: By setting boundaries with family and friends, you can avoid distractions and stay focused on what is important to you. This can help you manifest your goals more quickly and efficiently.

Reduce Stress and Anxiety: When you have healthy boundaries, you can reduce stress and anxiety in your life. This can help you stay calm and focused, which is essential for manifesting your goals.

Increase Self-Confidence: By setting boundaries and sticking to them, you can increase your self-confidence and feel more empowered. This can help you manifest your goals with greater ease and success.

Gratitude and its Role in Manifesting a Fulfilling Joyful Life

Gratitude is an important part of the manifestation journey. It helps us to focus on what we have and what we want, rather than what we lack or what we fear. When we practice gratitude, we are more likely to attract positive experiences and outcomes into our lives. Here are some ways in which gratitude can help us manifest our goals:

1. Shift Your Focus: When you focus on what you are grateful for, you shift your attention away from what you lack or fear. This helps to attract more positive experiences and outcomes into your life.
2. Increase Positive Emotions: Gratitude can increase positive emotions, such as joy, love, and contentment. This positive energy can help you manifest your goals with greater ease and success.
3. Boost Your Confidence: When you practice gratitude, you become more aware of your strengths and accomplishments. This can help build your confidence and believe in your ability to manifest our goals.
4. Attract Abundance: Gratitude is a powerful way to attract abundance into your life. When you are

grateful for what you have, you open yourself up to receive more blessings and opportunities.

5. Reduce Stress: Gratitude can also help reduce stress and anxiety. When you focus on the good in your life, you are less likely to worry about the future or dwell on the past. I remind myself consistently to be patient with myself and show myself the same grace and kindness that I show others.

Feel the Emotions, Take Action, And Manifest

Feeling your emotions fully and allowing yourself to process them is an important part of emotional wellbeing. However, it's also important to know when to move forward and take action towards your goals. Here are some steps you can take to feel your emotions fully and then move forward:

1. Allow Yourself to Feel Your Emotions: When you suppress your emotions, they can become trapped and lead to stress and anxiety. Take some time to sit with your emotions and feel them fully. This can be uncomfortable, but it's an important part of emotional processing.

2. Set a Time Limit: While it's important to feel your emotions fully, it's also important not to dwell on them for too long. Set a time limit, such as 10 to 20 minutes, to feel your emotions fully.

3. Take Action Towards Your Goals: Once you've allowed yourself to feel your emotions, it's time to

take action towards your goals. Plan for the next
step you need to take towards your goal and then
take that step.

4.   Practice Self-Care: Taking action towards your
goals can be challenging, so it's important to
practice self-care to help stay motivated and
focused. This can include things like exercise,
meditation, spending time with loved ones, or
engaging in a hobby.

Remember, it's okay to feel your emotions and take time to
process them. But at some point, you need to take action
towards your goals in order to create the life you want. By
allowing yourself to feel your emotions fully and then taking
action towards your goals, you can create a more fulfilling
and joyful life.

About Aruna Ramamurthy B. Sc., LMT, ISSA-CPT, NLPP

 Aruna Ramamurthy is a licensed medical massage therapist with 14 years of experience. She is also a yoga and trapeze instructor, Breath Coach, NLP Practitioner, Certified Life and Success Coach, and Clinical Hypnotherapist. She graduated from Madras University in India with a BS in Mathematics, Cincinnati School of Medical Massage, Yoga Teacher's College, and Transform Destiny.

Aruna is the founder of Enlighten Embody Empower Yourself LLC, which helps heart centered women entrepreneurs live a mindful, abundant, joyous life with inner peace while fulfilling their purpose.

Aruna is passionate about helping people reach their fullest potential and believes in the mind's power, body and soul. Through her unique approach to coaching, she has helped many find the courage and motivation to reach their goals.

Aruna is a highly sought-after speaker for her authenticity and is invited to speak at many conferences and seminars. She is an active member of many professional organizations.

To get Aruna's gift, visit:
www.BPABook.com/gift/Aruna

A Taste of Heaven

Tracie Ullman, NLPMP, MTT, MHt, MSC, EFT

Did you ever want to tell someone something so bad but knew if you did, you would risk being labeled a weirdo? I have heard a voice that wasn't mine speaking to me, protecting me, and helping me navigate through life since the age of six. But I didn't tell anyone about it. I thought they wouldn't believe a six-year-old, anyway. So, I hid it, stuffed it, lied about it, and kept it a secret.

Think about how hard that was at age 6. For long as I can remember, I have had this strong sense of intuition, and I can always tell when someone is lying to me. My stomach hurts badly, and I feel uneasy, and I'm shaky all over my body. I taught myself how to deal with this strong voice, now known as intuition, by limiting my gifts and never allowing others to penetrate my being.

I became a loner and isolated from others to the point of "diminishing my light" so I could just fit in with the masses. For instance, in school, I didn't really have to study hard. The lessons came easily to me. In fact, I stared out the window a lot. And because of my daydreaming, I was labeled "Spacie Tracie" even by my friends, something that hurt me a lot.

As I got older, I nurtured this gift, and as my feelings of empathy grew, it led me to a career in nursing. As a junior nurse in an ER, I certainly had my challenges with the more experienced nurses. I couldn't believe how negative and cruel they could be. Hiding supplies, hiding your pen so you couldn't chart, and switching your shifts to later hours without telling you were all part of the initiation process.

My unhealed trauma only compounded what was happening at work. I had suffered from sexual abuse as a child, my mother's personality disorder, and the separation and eventual divorce of my parents, only to be raised by my father's parents. I didn't realize at the time how unhealed trauma can affect your whole life. So, I quit the ER.

All I ever did when younger was apply fear and shame in my life. Something I learned from the elders who programmed me since being in the womb. After I had several debilitating meltdowns, loss of employment, and finally a near-death experience, was I ready to make a change.

Apply Positive Thoughts and Feelings Toward Desires

How many times in your life have you asked yourself, "How do I build confidence in myself to walk out of a job or relationship that is causing stress?" Or "How do I bring my gifts and talents to others so they can experience them while getting compensated too?"

These are good questions because you must have a burning desire. It's the desire that will keep you going and staying committed, no matter what. It's a way to care for others, not carry them, a way to observe others, not absorb them. YOU also need a plan. I didn't have one. I had to learn the hard way.

Being at Cause Emotionally, Mentally and Spiritually

But let me share with you the benefits of being at cause for your outcomes, because when you are in charge and at cause, you reclaim your personal power and subconsciously empower others to do the same. I am hoping the benefits I share will inspire you to act and stop making excuses once and for all.

Teach others you are entitled to hold on to your power and use it for personal benefit. Boundaries are important.

Help you acknowledge that you always have full responsibility for your life on all levels.

Eliminate feelings of restriction and limitation.

Prepare you for deciding through your heart.

Align you with your life purpose or spiritual path.

Transform your limiting beliefs & belief systems into more congruent ones that expand your possibilities.

Heal on all levels of human potential.

Increase your sense of peace and contentment.

Show you that you have more choices in any situation than you might previously have considered.

Restore feelings of expansiveness and creativity.

Enjoy the unlimited love that is available to you.

*A*ccept yourself that you are doing the best you can on any day.

*L*ive with love, gratitude, and integrity.

The path is real and right in front of you.

Part of spiritual awakening is mental freedom from possessions. By practicing non-attachment, you can enjoy life and perform material duties with a sense of service rather than of personal gain. The ego wants to cling to objects, ideas, youth, and other aspects of worldly experience. By letting go of these things gracefully when they have served their time, inner peace becomes strengthened.

Did I mention it took me 37 years to be spiritually awakened? Or that my ego can still get in the way? A good friend told me that if you are moving forward and not backwards, you're winning. Yes, some days it might not seem like you are winning, but you are.

You are winning because you showed up, suited up, stood up another day, and gave it your best. So, instead of asking yourself "Why am I here?" ask instead "Why am I the way I am?"

I ALWAYS FELT DIFFERENT. It never went away, no matter how I strived to be happy. Until one day, I devoted myself to a spiritual weekend that ultimately changed my life to a level of bliss unimaginable.

The Spiritual Weekend That Changed My Life

On a cold day in February 2010, outside of western Pennsylvania, I went to a sweat lodge with my husband, expecting to experience a higher consciousness of spirit. I had never heard of a sweat lodge and what it entailed. My husband arranged the stay, and I trusted him, and when life calls on you, you go.

I thought I was going to a warm lodge with cedar rooms, one where I would wear a soft white plush robe and cozy sippers. Afterward, I would be served hot tea with lemon and relax by a cozy fire with some short bread cookies.

There was a sense of excitement with a drop of nervousness upon arrival. Deep down, I knew I shouldn't be there, but I couldn't figure out why. When I saw the makeshift igloo of a lodge, I knew I had got myself into something that was going to be uncomfortable for me.

The lodge was made of twigs, blankets, and chicken wire, CLEARLY not what I had envisioned. There was an enormous fire pit right outside the front door of the lodge. In fact, the pit was bigger than the lodge, and I thought to myself, if a great wind stirred up, could the lodge catch fire? Why was this pit so close to the makeshift igloo looking thing?

Ignoring these thoughts, I stood outside and watched 22 others enter the lodge. I must have looked like a deer in headlights, wondering if I was going to fry up in this so-called sweat lodge. I remember thinking, I really don't want to do this, but I wanted to please my husband, even knowing he would have been totally fine if I didn't go in.

With minimal instructions given to us upon entering the lodge, we stripped down to our tank tops and shorts, no jewelry, hair was to be pulled back off our face and certainly no cell phones. It was 27 degrees outside; I was freezing and very uncomfortable standing there in my summer attire.

The others entered the lodge, and I had a problem with that. When my husband was going in, he asked me "What's the matter? You are not going to do it?" I said, "I can't go in there. I am sorry. I just can't."

The water pourer, Keith, oversaw the day. He asked me why I wasn't entering. I answered. He convinced me it was safe, so I entered. When I entered, I noticed immediately that my husband was sitting far from me. This made me anxious.

Looking back, I now know I needed to be alone with myself, so I felt comfortable enough to let go of my past trauma and all my fears. After all, I was a young mother with a 15-month-old baby, and I wanted to give him the best version of myself. After we were all in, the door closed, and it was so dark that I couldn't see my hand in front of my face.

The sage they lit reminded me of marijuana, and it gave me a sense of being high. The hot rocks glowed amber, so I tried to focus on them. We listened to Keith call in all ascended masters, ancestors, and spiritual guides to join us. I made it through a round of him chanting and humming "ohm".

I felt I could handle the next round, so when they opened the door to let fresh air in, I stayed for another journey. What happened next was life changing for me. My husband said I shouted out, "I need air!" The next thing I remember, I was lying outside the sweat lodge, and I could see my soul coming out of my body.

I was on my elbows and knees staring at my left arm, and I could see mist coming out of my arm. I drifted out of my body, and I felt so light. Looking down at my body, I wasn't bothered because I knew I was dying.

I floated away into the forest and was greeted by a man. He started off small at first and then grew into a larger being, wearing a white robe with a tan belt. He had brown hair that touched his shoulders, and he had the prettiest blue eyes I had ever seen. I felt very peaceful in his presence.

Even though he never introduced himself, I knew who he was. His name was Jesus. Without moving his lips and while looking deep into my eyes he said in my head, "Tracie, we are not here to judge you, we are here to do a review. How have you been compassionate to your fellow man?"

I was confused and shocked that he asked me that question. He knew I couldn't answer him even though I wanted to, so he showed me on a rock to the right of me, a vision of me being a safety guard in the 5th grade crossing over the 1st graders on Nelson Street in Allentown where I grew up.

He said, "You have always been compassionate towards others, even at an early age, but you make stuff up in your head of what you think they think of you. Others do not think those things of you, and you are going to go back, and you are going to serve them, and you are going to do great things in serving them."

There was no chance I was going to do that. My emotions said I am not going back to earth to serve them. So, I said to Jesus, "Serve them? Those people are so mean."

He replied, "You ARE going to go back, and you are going to do great things, and they will accept you with your gifts." Of course, I knew I would not get my way with him, so I changed my view and drifted from him.

I saw a mountain with a train on top of it and I knew I wanted to get that train. In that moment, between leaving Jesus and heading over to the train, I felt a presence of my angels. I could feel their love for me, and they were defending my desire to stay in heaven and not return to earth. They were even talking to Jesus, asking him to let me stay. He, of course, said "It's not her time."

My angels wanted nothing more than for me to be at peace and I will never forget how that felt, to feel so loved and supported. But before I returned to my body, I glimpsed the City of Jesus, where the departed children were.

I saw a hospital for the souls of the departed who overdosed on drugs, those who didn't know they were in heaven yet.

The angels said, "We have to transition them in slowly." And I heard the most beautiful music that earthly words cannot describe. I now understand today why I saw the hospital. It was so I could let go of the guilt of wanting to kill myself after my grandmother passed away from cancer.

I also understand why I saw the City of Jesus as I lost a child in my twenties because of a miscarriage. It devastated me and I grieved for that child for a long time. I saw a boy flying a kite in the City of Jesus, and I believe today that was my unborn son. It wasn't until I was 37 that I again conceived. I now have my baby boy, Jonah.

I remembered what Jesus said to me during my near-death experience: "You are going to go back, and you are going to serve them."

Serving After My Near-Death Experience

After my experience, I left nursing and became a Reiki Master, Master Hypnotherapist, NLP Trainer, Speaker, and opened my business.

I don't regret a single moment since opening SoulScapes Reiki Laser Skin Center in 2010, one year after my taste of heaven. It's a place where your soul can have an escape. It's a piece of heaven. My 5-star reviews on google say it all. It has been a journey and I am grateful that I am in a profession where I perceive my business through my heart and allow my love and compassion for others to shine.

About Tracie Ullman, NLPMP, MTT, MHt, MSC, EFT

 Tracie Ullman is a Hypnotherapist Empowerment Coach and Trainer with 15 years of experience. She graduated from Transform Destiny NLP Institute with a Major in Neuro Linguistic Programming and Hypnotherapy.

Tracie helps business owners, parents, and struggling salespeople make life easier and stress-free by helping them step out of their comfort zone. She has appeared on Ted X, Dr. Oz and hosted the Empower Hour Radio Show on WCHE Philadelphia.

Her dedication to her profession has been recognized with awards, most notably the Business of the Year in Chester County, Pennsylvania. She has also been featured in various publications, such as the Daily Local, Main Line Magazine, and The Reading Journal.

To get Tracie's book: It's Not Just A Facial, visit www.Tracieisullman.net/Tracie-Ullman

The 9 Keys to Manifesting

Lisa Ann Studer aka "The Queen of Manifestation"

My clients call me the "Queen of Manifestation". However, for years I felt like I was more of the Joker than the Queen. It was very frustrating because I was great at helping everyone else to manifest what they wanted. I was also very good at manifesting things when they benefited the people I loved and cared about. Yet, to manifest things for me, I just couldn't seem to get it to work.

In 2011, I had a health scare and had to have a procedure done. When I woke up the next morning, I was in a full-blown pity party. I was laying in bed crying my eyes out. I won't go into the entire story, but it is important to know that the health scare was just the icing on the cake of a disastrous few years.

The tears continued flowing uncontrollably, and I just kept thinking to myself, "what am I doing wrong"? Now I am not a perfect person, but honestly, there were murderers that seemed to have better luck in life than I was having. It was in that moment that everything would change.

You may call it intuition, your inner voice, a guide, an angel, or a higher power, but I literally heard a voice in my head that said, "What does your dream life look like?" That one question would forever change my life and set me on a journey to discover *The 9 Keys of Manifesting,* which eventually led me to becoming the Queen of Manifestation.

Manifesting is done through your thoughts.
Creating is done through your actions.

The 9 Keys to Manifesting

1. *Give Yourself Permission to Want What You Want*

Before we go any further, I want you to stop and think about what you would like to manifest in your life. Then I want you to ask yourself a very important question. When you ask yourself this question, you must be completely and totally honest with yourself. Ready? I want you to ask yourself if you truly feel deserving of having what you want.

Most people come from a place of lack. They believe that if they want more for themselves, they are being greedy, self-absorbed, and egotistical. People will say things like, "I should just be happy with what little I have" or "other people have it worst". Yes, that may be true, but guess what? There are many people who have it a lot better! We seem to have a lot easier time talking ourselves into settling as opposed to allowing ourselves to feel deserving.

The next question is one that changed my life! Have you ever asked yourself what *your* dream life looks like? If you are like most people, you are busy dealing with all the stuff you don't want in your life. You are trying to cope, keep up, and figure out the solution to the problems. Honestly, who has time to be thinking about a dream life when they are buried under bills, in a poor relationship, struggling with health issues, in an unsatisfying job, etc.? However, it is

112

exactly in that moment that you need to take a step back and ask yourself that question.

Let's try something. I want you to imagine that there is a big red pause button right in front of you. Now I want you to imagine hitting that button. Hit it! Now I want you to *allow* yourself to think about what your dream life would look like. See it, feel it, hear it, and allow yourself to truly experience it as if it is in the moment of now!

2. Be Really Willing to Receive

Over the years, I have literally worked with thousands of people. During that time, I have learned that there are two simple reasons most people cannot manifest what they truly want in their lives.

One we already addressed, because they do not feel deserving. The second one is because they are unwilling to receive when things do not unfold in a way that is comfortable. Many times, our opportunities come disguised as challenges, so we are unwilling to accept them. We cannot allow ourselves to see beyond that moment. We are unwilling to receive.

Years ago, I had a friend who absolutely hated her job. She called me every day to tell me how much she hated it. I heard about this job so much that I started hating it and I didn't even work there. I would constantly ask her why she wasn't looking for another job. It seemed like a simple solution. Yet, no matter how many times I asked, she always brought the conversation back to how miserable she was.

One day, she called me crying hysterically. I honestly thought something had happened to one of her children. Through the tears and heavy breathing, she blurted out, "I lost my job today and I am so completely devastated." She kept saying that she didn't understand why this happened to *her*.

I really tried to muster up every ounce of compassion, but I honestly could not figure out why she was so upset. I gently and lovingly reminded her of how much she hated the job and how long she had been complaining about it.

She eventually got over her devastation, found another job that she loved, and then continued to tell me how she regretted staying at the other job for so long.

Sometimes we need to let go of one thing before the next can appear. When trying to manifest, we must be willing to receive, even when an opportunity may not present itself in the way we think it should. We must be strong and brave and willing to allow things to unfold in their own way and in their own time. We need to remember that growth happens outside of our comfort zone.

3. Be Clear on Your Why

Grab a pen and write this down. *I cannot manifest something that involves the actions of another.* You cannot manifest your dad quitting smoking or your ex's new love dumping him. You cannot manifest your boss being transferred to Alaska (Not that there is anything wrong with Alaska. I hear it is absolutely beautiful there).

When manifesting, you must be clear on your why? Why do you want to manifest that thing? When you are trying to manifest, it must align with your highest good. You may really want that ex back, but if they are truly not good for you, it will not work! It really is that simple.

4. Stay in a High Vibration

Did you know our thoughts and feeling have a frequency? Just like sound and light, our thoughts vibrate through our mind. In fact, all things in our universe are constantly in motion, vibrating.

It lifts our vibration when we are in a place of peace and happiness. But when we are focusing on all our problems, it keeps us in a place of fear and negativity, thus lowering our vibration. You need to keep yourself in the highest state possible when trying to manifest.

Stay out of the fear and negativity. Stop asking how and when. Instead, stay focused on what you are trying to manifest. Remember the question, what does my dream life look like? Continually ask yourself that question.

5. Take Inspired Action

I can't tell you how many times clients come to me talking about how they want a new job, a better relationship, a healthier lifestyle, more money, etc. When I ask them what they are doing to make what they want to happen, I get responses that include things like I am meditating on it, I put it on my dream board, and I have affirmations on sticky notes all over my house.

Now, those are all great things, and they will help you stay focused on what you are working on manifesting. However, you MUST take action to truly bring what you want to you.

If you want a new job, start sending out resumes. Want a better relationship? Maybe try some counseling to see why you are attracting the wrong relationship, and then go out and start dating. If you want a healthier lifestyle, grab a friend, and start walking, hire a coach, join a gym, take a class, or read a book on nutrition. Desire for more money? Then start educating yourself about money and finances.

You need to act! You need to take inspired action! Get excited! Get inspired! Make the journey of manifesting an exciting one.

6. Trust Your Soul's Path

As I tell my kids, all the time, if happiness and success were easy, everyone would experience it. It takes work! Yet, most people do not realize it is a lot easier than they think and it can be fun work! Now, when you hit those moments of doubt and you question your ability to manifest, or maybe you are a little negative, take a step back and ask yourself these questions:

A. *How is this helping me positively?*
There is never a moment in your life when thinking negatively will be helpful! Trust me on this. If you find yourself in this place, shift your focus and get out of that negative thought process.

B. *What is the worst-case scenario?*
Whenever I have a huge and scary decision to make, I always ask myself this question. Ironically, the answer is never as bad as I think it is. For most people, the worst-case scenario is that they fail, and they do not get what they are trying to manifest.

Great, then the worst thing that happens is you are exactly where you started. Oh, and by the way, here is a little manifesting secret from yours truly. There is no such thing as failure, only what I like to call re-routing points.

C. *When I look back on this 10-years from now, will I regret not trying?*
After working with people for so many years, I have learned many valuable things. One of the most important things that I have learned is that the biggest regrets people have are over the things they did NOT do!

When you are thinking of doing something new, manifesting what you want, and fear and doubt come in, just ask yourself, "Will I look back on this 10-years from now and regret not trying?"

7. *Mantra Magic*

A mantra is a word or phrase you repeat (often used in meditation) as a tool to help you release your mind. It is a wonderful way to help you bring awareness and focus, as well as letting go of any negative emotions or thoughts you may be experiencing. Here are some of my favorite mantras that keep me in the manifesting magic!

- I am in transition to success.
- I am exactly where I need to be.
- I am a wonderful being of light.
- The only one who needs to believe in me is ME.

You can use these mantras or have fun creating new ones just for yourself!

8. *Pick Who You Share Your Dreams With*

This is a lesson I have had to learn the hard way more times than I wish to admit. I remember back in the day when I was trying to manifest a healthy and happy relationship. Looking back, I realized I was always surrounding myself with people who didn't believe a happy and healthy relationship was possible. I was part of what I now like to call the "all men stink, and no one is ever happy in a relationship" club.

When you are focusing on manifesting, you need to be careful who you share your dreams with. A friend going through a messy divorce is not a good choice for a support person when you are trying to manifest a healthy and happy relationship. The person who can never keep a job and has no money is not the go-to person for financial advice. It is always best to take advice and align yourself with the people who are already experiencing what you want to experience.

9. Do YOUR Inner Work

A client once asked me, "When do you think I will be done working on myself?" I looked at him, smiled, and said, "When you are dead."

We are always a work in progress. We are always learning, growing, and sharing! I truly believe that we are like an onion. As we move through the layers, we are constantly releasing things we no longer need to hold on to and tapping into our true abilities and talents.

Everyone is intuitive.

Everyone has healing abilities.

Everyone has the power to create the life they want and deserve to have.

Always remember that you are a beautiful being of light and are truly deserving of living your dream life.

Happy Manifesting!

About Lisa Ann Studer aka "The Queen of Manifestation"

 Lisa Ann is an Internationally known Psychic Medium, and Intuitive Healer. She is Board Certified through the International Board of Coaches and Practitioners and holds the following credentials: NLP Practitioner, Success & Life Coach, Clinical Hypnotherapist, Time Techniques Practitioner, and EFT Practitioner. She is also Certified as a Holistic Life Coach, Reiki Master Teacher, and received her Past Life Regression Certification directly from Brian Weiss.

Lisa Ann is the published author of the books *No Phones in Heaven* and *Past Lives - Have I Been Here Before?* She is the creator of 3 Guided Meditation CD's *Angelic Whispers*, *Body Mind Spirit,* and *Create Your Reality.* She also has her own line of Essential Oils, called Spiritscents.

Lisa Ann hosted her own TV show *Create Your Reality*, was the lead Psychic on the TV show *Scared*, co-hosted two Radio shows *The Paranormal Outsider* and *Walt & LA Live*, and has been a guest on several TV and Radio shows, as well as having her work featured in several books.

She began her career in NY in 1995 and founded Spiritquest in 1999. In 2013, she moved to NC and met her husband Kyle (a massage therapist). Today Spiritquest is a full-service Body Mind Spirit Spa & Gift Shop which they run together.

Get a gift from Lisa Ann: www.BPAbook.com/gift/Lisa

The Power of Intentional Living

Michelle Duffy, MBA, NLPMP, MTT, CMHt, MSC

As the sunset and the stars and moon grew brighter, the four of us gazed out my big bedroom window. I kneeled, as I often do, to feel closer to my three children: William, nine, and the twins Emily and James, six. We watched as the pink, orange, and red hues in the sky faded into darkness.

I took a deep breath and intentionally committed each of their smiling faces to memory. Then, I asked them, "Do you feel it?" William replied, "Feel what, Mama?" "This. The present moment." I said. My children exchanged smiles, familiar with my odd talks about the mind, body, and soul connection.

This **intentional living** technique helps me to drop into my heart, set an intention, and feel the intense emotions while "cataloging" the memory in a special place in my mind. Later, I can quickly access it to raise my vibrations when needed. This practice is straightforward yet powerful, and you can effortlessly incorporate it into your life.

Contrary to popular belief: you don't need *big* changes, just little ones that, when done, *deliberately* and *continually,* drastically alter your life.

A Practical Definition

Now, let's define **intentional living**. According to Wikipedia, it's a "lifestyle based on an individual or group's conscious attempts to live according to their values and beliefs". I've found the concept to be much deeper than this.

Intentional Living Has Four Elements:
1. Being aware of who you are which helps you know *what your* heart's desires, beliefs, and values are.
2. Choosing to consciously and deliberately be present and more responsible for directing your life and not living on "autopilot".
3. Setting a positive **intention** which helps you direct your energy and efforts in a specific direction.
4. Knowing the purpose behind everything you do, your big *why* in life.

The Wikipedia definition encompasses the first element but leaves out the rest. Without being in the moment, you being aware of your desires, values, and beliefs will seem like a distant thing. Your power in *living* those values and beliefs is acknowledging and savoring the human joy of just being in the here and now.

Without having an **intention** of living your life with those beliefs and values, you'll find your energy going in different directions and not deliberately focusing on what your desires are.

Finally, without knowing your purpose in life, it is hard to continue to live by your beliefs and values when you hit a "wall"- as we all do.

Now, let's clarify **intention**. The dictionary says it is an aim or plan. I believe that <u>intention focuses and carries the energy of your manifestation.</u> Energy is who you truly are, and it's also yours to use at your command. Where you put your mind, your energy goes, and energy carries information.

If your intention is ecological (meaning good for you, others, and the planet) then your manifestation will bring in abundance, whereas an intention that is not will only bring about destruction. That's why Hitler's movement grew, but because the intention was not pro-survival for all, it had an imminent, appalling end.

<u>Neuroplasticity, The Science Behind Intentional Living</u>

Let me explain why understanding the science is vital. I want your logical mind to understand and agree with the scientific basis of intentional living. To effectively apply this knowledge, I suggest that you first convince your conscious mind to support it.

Then you can review the principles involved with your subconscious mind (where your beliefs and habits live). <u>This approach aligns both your conscious and subconscious minds so that your subconscious beliefs and habits support your conscious desires.</u> Ultimately, this alignment will help you achieve your goals more easily.

Studies have shown that neuroplasticity plays a key role in enhancing human cognition, which refers to the ability to engage in goal-oriented behaviors rather than merely reacting to the present moment. This is achieved through **training and intensive practice**. In the example of meditation, one study discovered that *regular practice* helps people concentrate more easily and live in the present moment. Meditation is one of many practices that can be used to live intentionally.

Neuroplasticity refers to the brain's ability to change its neuron connections, allowing for behavioral change. This is called "rewiring" the brain. It's important to note that intelligence is not fixed from birth. Your brain continues to grow through learning, changes in mindset, and social connections. This scientific understanding is empowering because it highlights the fact that *you* are in control of your own mind!

The subconscious mind (which holds your beliefs, habits, and memories) handles 95% of your decision-making. For instance, if you consciously aspire to become wealthy, but your subconscious beliefs contradict this goal by viewing rich individuals as dishonest, it will hinder you from achieving it. That's why it's crucial to align your conscious and subconscious so you can effectively manifest what you want.

Awareness is always the first step toward change. You're now aware of how the mechanism works to override it.

Neuroplasticity applies to intentional living because it's up to *you* to redefine where you focus your energy, be

124

conscious of the beliefs that are holding you back in order to drive new behavior and create the habits you desire.

One Decision Alone *Can* Change Your Life.

When I was in my twenties, I, like many people my age, had a strong desire to be accepted. Even though I had already had my first moment of awakening at age 15, I was still very immature. I turned to alcohol because it gave me confidence. I became a huge party girl and did many things I now regret.

Yet, in my moments of sobriety, I discovered meditation and reading anything metaphysics. This gave me hope and happiness. One night, I cried upon realizing that the more people liked me, the more it wasn't *me*. It was not the first time I had been going through a "dark night of the soul" period in my life. The only difference was that when I was fourteen, I looked sad, but this time I was deceivingly joyful. This experience reminds me to be kind to others, since their appearance may not reflect their inner turmoil.

One day as I lay crying on my bathroom floor (as usual) and feeling sorry for myself (again)... something clicked within me. I shouted, "I'm tired of this! This is *not* who I want to be!" and a voice inside me said: "Then don't."

In an instant, everything felt peaceful. The words sank in as I held myself. I took a deep breath and finally smiled, realizing I had fallen "asleep" in my life. So, I said in my mind, "I forgive myself. I forgive myself for not remembering who I

am." Then I felt strong and confident as I simply *decided* that I was going to **live intentionally** awake and aware of the present moment.

Deliberately Applying the Knowledge

Neuroplasticity shows that you're not limited by your current conditioning. You *can* change the connections in your brain to align with your new goals and intentions. The process to apply the knowledge is:

Step 1. Become aware of who you are. You have a unique purpose in your life, and part of that purpose is to discover your true self. By understanding who you are, you'll be able to identify your heart's desires. If you're unsure about your true self, don't worry. Many people are in the same boat.

Start small by making deliberate choices about simple things, like choosing a restaurant to go to, and then work your way up to bigger decisions. In no time, you'll just *know* who you are and what you want.

Step 2. Practice being the "observer" of your thoughts and beliefs. Don't judge them. Simply observe them for a week. This allows you to see how many negative things you're telling yourself or you believe in. This **awareness** allows you to question if those stories are even true.

Step 3. Once you know what you really want, ask yourself *why* you actually want that. Ask yourself at least five times to get into the deeper why. Your "why" - the reason behind your actions - will help you persevere through difficult times. What you do in life isn't as important as doing it with purpose.

It's not *what* you do, but *how* you do it. So, people who act with purpose are happy and unstoppable, regardless of their job. For this reason, it's essential for you to search relentlessly for your "why" because it *will* serve as your motivation in all that you do.

<u>Step 4. Set an intention.</u> You can use intention setting for everything. Set an intention for a new relationship, a new project, the beginning of a new day, etc. Once you know what you want out of that situation or person, you can then declare the intention by writing it down, saying it out loud, or in your mind. If the intention is planned in a way that the subconscious mind grasps, it *will be effective.*

The subconscious mind operates uniquely, and it follows specific rules. One of these rules is that it doesn't comprehend negatives. For example, if I say, "don't think about a pink elephant," it's impossible for you not to think of one. Additionally, the subconscious mind only understands present tense. Keeping these two rules in mind will enhance the power of your intentions.

Instead of saying, "I don't want my day to be terrible," try saying, "My intention for today is to approach everything with an open heart." Notice that by avoiding negative words, the **intention** carries a more positive vibration, which strengthens it. The words you choose are not the only factor; *the tone and emotions you use are equally important.*

Step 5. Practice makes progress. Continue to come back to the present moment fully whenever you catch yourself being on autopilot. It takes time and deliberate practice, but it's also not rocket science. Let's not make it seem impossible (time to stop fighting for your limitations). You *can* do this!

Step 6. This is *THE* most important part of the process: DECIDE NOW! If you've read this far and feel a sense of truth that you've been living unconsciously and unaware, it's time for you to decide. Like when I decided during that rock-bottom moment to stop living that way. *A firm and definite decision is all you need to make.*

The question is: Will you continue living without awareness of your purpose or aspirations, operating on autopilot? Or will you finally declare, "Enough! I choose me!"

<u>Regaining Your Power to Live Intentionally</u>

Have you realized that the amount of information we receive has drastically increased in the last decade? This surge in information, also known as "infobesity," is not just about quantity but also about the quality of the data we consume. It can lead to heightened stress and anxiety levels, as most messages we receive are negative or geared towards promoting consumerism. It's no wonder that many of us struggle with self-confidence, focus, and self-love.

Infobesity also distracts us from dealing with our emotions. We numb ourselves by engaging in overeating, over drinking, binge-watching, endlessly scrolling on social media, or even turning to hard drugs. These coping mechanisms turn us into unconscious robotic versions of ourselves. We lose touch with our inner self and the power to create.

Living intentionally *is* an antidote to this unconsciousness and the importance of choosing this way of living cannot be understated.

Living intentionally means being conscious and present throughout your day, allowing you to observe your thoughts, words, and behaviors. When you are the "observer", you can distance yourself from negative stories or beliefs that can take you on a downward spiral of hopelessness. By recognizing the lies of your ego mind, you regain your power and can choose what to focus on, acting from a place of inner *knowingness* and unconditional love.

Intentional living is not a magic solution, but it is a way of life that you can start practicing **right now** to become more aware and ignite change in your life. As you become more **intentional**, you'll awaken a desire to help others and humanity. This process will lead to major shifts in your perception and guidance toward the next levels of your life.

About Michelle Duffy, MBA, NLPMP, MTT, CMHt, MSC

 Michelle has an in-depth understanding of the power of NLP, hypnotherapy, and metaphysical principles and uses her expertise to help her clients create profound and lasting change.

She holds a degree in Industrial Engineering and uses her knowledge to develop customized programs that validate spiritual principles with science. Her courses concentrate on aligning the conscious mind (analytical) with the subconscious mind (beliefs) to achieve congruency. This alignment results in remarkable and long-term outcomes for clients, including releasing anxiety and stress, processing negative beliefs, living in the present moment, and understanding how to navigate the game of life.

Michelle is especially passionate about helping mothers know how to regulate their nervous system proactively, so they come from a place of compassion and intuition needed to raise happy, self-determined, and confident children.

Her mission is to help others reach their highest potential and live a life full of abundance, purpose, and joy. If you're looking for guidance, support, and a renewed sense of purpose, you can trust Michelle to help you create profound and lasting change.

To get Michelle's gift, visit:
www.BPABook.com/gift/Michelle

Asking the Right Questions to be Positively Awesome

Amanda Scott, MA, LCPC, NCC

You may have noticed the inner dialog, often referred to as self-talk, running through your mind. Without sufficient mindfulness, this self-talk or self-story can easily lead you to ask yourself questions you do not really want the answer to.

You may ask yourself: Why am I so stupid? What is wrong with me? Why don't things ever work out? Why am I always disappointed by others? No answers to these questions will help one become positively awesome. In fact, it is much more likely for these answers to create a negative thinking spiral that lowers motivation and self-esteem.

I know you are now wondering what to do about this inner dialog. The answer is not to stop the dialog or to stop asking yourself questions—that would be impossible. It is better to be more mindful about the questions you are asking. With practice, this shift in the questions asked will become automatic.

Let us revisit the previous example questions. When you ask yourself: why am I so stupid? Your brain will generate ideas and examples of situations where you made less than intelligent choices. By asking yourself: What is wrong with me? You will generate many ideas and situations of you falling short of your expectations. You ask: Why don't things ever work out? Your brain again collects all the data for all the things not working out. You wonder: Why am I always disappointed by others? Once again, the mental generator is reminding yourself of all the ways others have disappointed you. I am sure you are noticing a pattern. Asking these questions leads to disturbing examples, which lead to a negative spiral of thinking.

The Negative Thinking Traps

What is meant by a negative thinking spiral? There are common, unhelpful thinking traps that lead into each other, creating a negative and intense emotional response. The following are some common examples of these thinking traps:

All-or-Northing Thinking—viewing a situation in extreme terms, unable to recognize the middle ground or middle terms.

Magnification/Catastrophizing—exaggerating the likely impact a situation will have or viewing a situation as a catastrophic event, though it is not.

Negative Filtering—discounting or ignoring all the positives and only giving attention to the negatives.

Jumping to Conclusions—assuming negative consequences or outcomes with no evidence to support assumptions.

Emotional Reasoning—mistaking an emotional response for factual interpretation.

Personalization—blaming yourself for all negative events, taking ownership of factors beyond your control and/or not holding others accountable.

Blame—the opposite of personalization, where you blame others or the universe and do not hold yourself accountable for the factors within your control.

Labeling—identifying the whole self with defective description rather than label the behavior/decision as defective.

"Should" Statements—you turn your preferences into rigid rules and experience extreme disappointment and frustration when those preferences are not met.

Asking the wrong questions can trigger these thinking traps, and the majority also feed into each other, crushing your motivation to be positive. If the questions you ask can be so powerful, it makes sense to be mindful of the questions that you are asking, does it not? By simply changing your questions, you can unlock a whole new perspective on life.

Rather than asking: Why am I so stupid? You want to try: How can I be more mindful? Instead of searching for what is wrong with myself; ask: What do I need to be more effective? Or ask: What are my strengths?

Avoid the trap of wondering why things never work out and shift to: How have things worked out? Or even: What can I learn from this?

It is ineffective to ask why others are such a disappointment when you can ask: What do others need to be more effective? What additional information does the other person need?

Words have power, so be mindful of what you are thinking, so you can use them positively.

The Science Simplified

I would like to take a moment to discuss some of the science and biology of these brain processes. It is important to recognize that the brain has a natural, healthy tendency to generalize, delete, and distort the incoming information so you can make the world a mentally more manageable place.

The mind generalizes to find the commonalities in situations and better predicts how to respond. For instance, we generalize that all red octagons on street corners mean to stop. We delete needless information such as the sound of the air vent or exactly how many cars we see from point one to point two. This deletion is very important to leave room in our conscious awareness of the truly important information—like the smoke alarm or the weaving car.

We distort to allow information to fit with our current beliefs; like the love-goggles we wear in a new relationship, and we cannot see any negatives in the new love interest. These processes are usually very helpful and, occasionally, are also what help create the thinking traps in the negative thinking spiral.

To keep this science section simple, we can focus on just a few areas of the brain and their roles in all of this. First, there is a system of nerve cells and fibers located deep within the upper part of the brain stem, called the reticular activating system. This system controls alertness and consciousness projecting into and stimulating areas of the cortex. Simply put, this area works as a gatekeeper, deciding what information will alert in consciousness and what information will go ignored.

To put this in another perspective, the reticular activating system has an awareness of one hundred percent of what is happening around you and filters it down to less than one percent. I am sure you now understand why the brain must generalize, delete, and distort to better organize all this information and select such a small percentage to send to conscious awareness.

Second, the prefrontal cortex regulates thoughts, actions, emotions, reasoning, problem-solving, comprehension, impulse control, creativity, and persistence. Together, the reticular activating system selects the information that is brought to awareness and the cortex regulates how the information is interpreted and what is done with it. Again, we see the generalizations, the deletions, and the distortions arise with the cortex's interpretation of the information. The cortex uses your experience to guide how to interpret incoming information.

The third important piece to this thinking puzzle is the billions of neurons present within the body and brain, with the highest numbers in the brain and spinal cord. Neurons act as information highways between the areas of the brain and body. Neurons take up and send out electrical and chemical signals leading to thought formation. There is an expression in the mental health field: *neurons that fire together, wire together*. Meaning we can reinforce a pattern of negative thinking or a pattern of positive thinking, making the thought pattern habitual and automatic.

These areas, along with others not mentioned, lead to the process of confirmation bias and what we know as the Law of Attraction.

Confirmation bias is the tendency for the brain to filter information or interpret it to support your current beliefs or theory about a topic. So, if you are believing and questioning why everything is awful, your brain will filter the information, so only awful things come to your consciousness and it will prove you correct in your theory.

However, if you switched your theory to questioning what can go well; your brain will filter the incoming information to bring the positives into your conscious awareness, leading to the Law of Attraction.

The Law of Attraction is more of a spiritual nature than the brain process and operates on a similar principle as confirmation bias. It is a belief that if your thoughts are negative, then you will attract a negative experience. The opposite is also true. If your thoughts are positive, then you will attract positive experiences.

Biologically speaking, these areas exist, so why not use them to your advantage? Don't you agree?

The Goal of Questions

This brings us to the most important point of the chapter: How to ask the right questions for a positively awesome mindset? Having read this far means you are ready for change. In a word, the answer for this change is intent.

You want to set your questions the same way you want to set goals: focusing on the wanted outcome rather than focusing on the unwanted. Asking questions that focus on what you want helps you connect with your desired intent. When you ask why a situation or action did not work out, it only mentally connects you to the negative outcome and sparks up the negative thinking neural pathways. So, asking how to make things work or how to make a situation better will connect you more to what you want.

It is also beneficial to recognize that your negative thought patterns get caught in a judgment trap. The judging mind rarely serves you; more often, it is your judgements that lead to the negative thought spiral. This spiral narrows your focus and you become boxed in with your problems. Slowly, there feels like no escape and no other options for dealing with what may upset you. However, when you are focused on what you want, it helps you to stop judging what the present moment is not and start getting curious about how to appreciate or improve the present moment. By remaining open and curious, you allow for more space for new information. Suddenly, there appear to be more options, there are more escape paths available, and you no longer feel boxed in.

Putting It All Together

Whether you think of it as confirmation bias, the Law of Attraction, or a new neural pathway to make habitual, you should now clearly see you can trust your subconscious mind.

I want to leave you with examples of effective questions to ask to help you on your journey of becoming positively awesome. In many questions, I use the word "*this*" referring to the problem or situation that may have led you to your previous patterns of ineffective questions that lead to the negative thinking spiral.

How can I be more mindful?

What can I learn from *this*?

How can I move past *this*?

What additional information do I need about *this*?

What strength can I use for *this*?

What part of *this* is working?

Which part of *this* can I change?

148

What do I need?

What do I want?

How are they viewing *this*?

What do they need to better help with *this*?

How can I communicate *this* better?

How can I view *this* differently?

As you trust in the process, you will find - with the right questions to guide you, you shift your mindset to a motivating state. Your mind knows exactly what to do and can do whatever it takes any time you allow it. The more you ask the questions you want the answers to, the more your thinking patterns will guide you to how to get what you want and guide you to take effective action.

You are changing all the time. What would it be like for you to have the change you seek so easily?

About Amanda Scott, MA, LCPC, NCC

 Amanda Scott is a Licensed Clinical Professional Counselor over 15 years of experience in education and counseling. She is currently employed at GreenPath Clinic, Dayrise Wellness, and Park Ridge Psychological Services.

Amanda has a wealth of knowledge and experience to help individuals navigate life's transitions, identify and reach personal potential, and create and accomplish goals. She is a Certified Clinical Anxiety Treatment Professional, Certified ADHD Professional, Licensed Professional Educator, and Learning Behavioral Specialist.

Amanda is passionate about providing her clients with the best care possible and her ability to connect with her clients on a personal level has been a great asset in helping them on their path to self-discovery and development. She has a strong commitment to helping individuals reach their potential and live a full and meaningful life.

Through her professional experience and training, Amanda is able to provide her clients with the tools they need to make positive and lasting changes in their lives. She is dedicated to helping her clients reach their fullest potential and discover their true selves.

To get Amanda's gift, e-book Quotes for Action, visit: www.BPABook.com/gift/Amanda

How to Get Slim and Trim Without Crazy Diets and Brutal Exercises

Helen Fong, CCHt, NLPP, PTT, CSC, EFT

Forty years ago, my mom was only 100 pounds and 40 years old when we immigrated from a poor village in China to Canada. For other parts of the world, women over forty gain weight. That was not the case for my mom. She was not sick, and she wasn't choosing not to eat.

It was because there was not enough food for her four starving children and herself. She allowed us to eat first while she barely had enough. Fortunately, her challenging time ended once we landed in Canada.

Looking back, everyone I knew in my village was skinny and slim. Back then, if you had a little extra weight, you were well fed and wealthy. We never had to go on a diet, nor had I ever heard of anyone needing to exercise to lose weight.

In Canada, however, real and fake food is everywhere and is easily accessible. Highly preserved food and GMOs are overeaten and people are getting sick. Then pharmaceutical companies jump in to create the drugs to keep us alive.

I felt the pressure of fake food and society's standards as I approached 50 years old. I was perceived as old and worried about the rumors of losing my sexual drive, lack of intimacy, and all those things that society claims come with aging.

And I felt the pressure to maintain a certain standard and to really take nutrition and exercises to the next level. Never in a million years did I imagine I would step onto a bikini fitness competition stage at this point in my life.

I guess the desire to feel valued, vital, and attractive again propelled me to do something audacious. I knew that staying the same would be more painful and dangerous than stepping out there to make some risky choices.

Now I will share with you some of the crazy findings and discoveries in my journey from having an average looking 50 years old body to build this bikini fitness figure. One that got 1st, 2nd, and 3rd place in multiple bikini fitness competitions, even competing among women half of my age.

What I discovered is that our body is an ever-changing organism you can alter and sculpt anyway you wish. You have full control of it and genetics do not have as much influences as many assume.

I believe our environment meaning how much, what, and when we put food in our body matters more. When you apply these findings in your body toning journey, you will discover how simple it is to achieve your ideal body.

Your body is a beautiful piece of art given to you by your parents. Perhaps while being a mom, wife, or busy professional, you got caught up taking care of others and forgot to pay attention to yourself.

Here are some things that you must do, and avoid, to get slim and trimmed and have fun pursuing your dream body. You will be amazed how little you need to change with your diet and training to have that young looking figure even at age 50, and beyond.

There are only three components that you need to dive into in this transformation: exercise, recovery, and nutrition. Let us start with exercise.

First, you don't need to spend hours in the gym. All you need is to stimulate your muscles enough to grow. Muscles only get stronger and strengthened with pressure and resistance. If your muscles never get sore while you're in the gym, then they are not being stimulated enough to change.

Contrary to myths, we do not lose muscles as we age. If you are a mom who breastfeed your children, you probably know what I mean. Your body, including muscles, continues to change when you demand it. When your baby continues to demand your breastmilk, your body will continue making it.

Here is another example to illustrate how amazing and capable our bodies are to stimulus. I was told that our female structures are like a campfire. The fire will keep going as long as you keep feeding it with wood, the flame will continue.

Once a Chinese medicine doctor reminded me that a female's body can experience many orgasms at a time and the more stimulated she gets, the more aroused she is... her body is like an oven. Of course, this is a mind and body connection as well. The good news is that with NLP, I believe we can still look and feel amazing at any age.

Second, most women are mistaken that they will look bulky if they weight lift. They may if they take drugs, otherwise it is difficult because women have much lower muscle building hormones than men.

Instead of worrying about being bulky, think of building muscles like investing in a property that generates passive income. With powerful muscles, your body continues to melt off fat even when you are at rest watching TV.

So, instead of running and walking for hours or doing aerobics, invest in resistance training. Resistance training promotes muscle growth. Aerobics are good, but it's like working from paycheck to paycheck. What you need is to invest in training smart to ensure your muscles are being stimulated to grow.

Third, understand energy used for exercise is not created inside your body, but it is transferred. When your body needs energy, and when the energy is not from food, your body uses fat as a source of energy. Therefore, when you eat more than what your body uses, your body will not use your body fat as energy. So, eat only as needed to protect your vital organs. We'll get into this more when we talk about nutrition.

Now to look at recovery starting with sleep. During proper sleep, your body releases hormones which help in the fat melting process. You might also recognize that muscles in your body are like babies that grow during sleep. So, getting great sleep is one of the simplest methods to lose body fat, given the proper nutrition and training.

No matter your age, your muscles grow upon demand, contrary to old beliefs that as we age, our muscles stop growing. Have you ever breastfed your child and notice how your body keeps on producing milk until your child no longer needs it, then your body stops producing it? Older people stop putting more effort into the gym, so their muscles go away. With effort, proper nutrition, stimulation, and recovery, muscles grow upon demand. Isn't this amazing that you can have beautiful muscles like an old car can have a new engine and a new interior?

Remember, muscles need some love to change. They must be fed with good nutrition and the rest to grow. In addition, you must protect your muscles from toxin substances. Research has shown that when cells are placed in an environment where there are toxins, the cells are closed, whereas when the cells are placed in an environment with good nutrients, these cells open up and grow.

One way I loved my muscles was to change my lifestyle of alcohol consumption. I discovered that most athletes don't consume alcohol because alcohol disrupts the fat burning power and the muscle formation process.

So, eat and drink for energy and muscle building more than for satisfaction. When you eat for energy, you will feel better and when you eat to build muscles, you will look better. And that brings us to the most important component, nutrition.

First, you must understand your metabolism. Most people just eat without knowing how their body processes the food. So, when there's weight gain, it must be genetics, not what is eaten, right?

Do you know someone who eats as much as you do and hardly puts on any weight, even though your lifestyles are quite the same? Chances are your body structure is different and perhaps you might have a small body structure with smaller and thinner bones and muscles.

With more muscles and bigger body frames, more energy is required to move it around. Therefore, a slice of bread with 100 calories gets burned off in a bigger individual with leaner muscle mass quicker than a slice of bread in someone whose body frame has lower muscle mass.

You also need to understand that calories are not created equal. A 200 calories muffin is not the same as 200 calories from a piece of chicken breast. Research has shown individuals in a group with the higher calories lost more body fat and gain more muscles than a group given fewer calories. Of course, the group with more calories was given quality food versus the lower calories from more processed foods.

Which brings us to the myth that most people think you have to eat like a rabbit to get slim and trim. It is the opposite. You must eat even when you do not feel like it because you are not eating for yourself but for preservation and protection of your vital organs.

This is contrary to what most people do when they want to lose weight. They starve themselves. Starving shuts down your metabolism, which means lower your fat burning potential, which weakens your vital organs.

Restricting too many calories and nutrients lowers your overall energy level, which will prevent you from being physically and mentally active.

Instead of restricting calories, choose food that has a thermic effect, meaning food that uses more of your body energy to process them. For example, eating raw and less processed food like vegetables requires your body to use more energy to break them down and deliver to the rest of your body.

Imagine what happens when you put some food in your food processor. How much energy does it take to blend some eggs and oils versus meat and fibers? You get the picture. Imagine your body as the food blender. Imagine 100 calories from two pieces of chocolate versus 100 calories from a handful of vegetables. How long does it take your body to digest the vegetables and the chocolate? You must chew the vegetables and chewing takes energy.

And don't forget to keep track of what you eat. It is very difficult to outwork your food. A big burger, a large fry, and soda or latte probably have thousands of calories, which might take you hours and hours in the gym to burn it off.

So, just because you spend 30 minutes on a treadmill doesn't mean you shall have an all you can eat buffet, hoping your body can take care of all your food like a garbage disposal. Whatever your body doesn't use as energy, your body keeps it and stores it as body fat. So, be aware of what you're eating and drinking.

And understand the difference between body weight and body fat. Most people mistake body fat as body weight. Your body weight includes all your hair, teeth, muscles, bones, while body fat is the fat that looks bumpy behind your thighs, around your arms, and in your midsection.

What happens when you lose weight by lowering your calories? You might not be protecting your vital organs from functioning, and they become weaker, which leads to lower metabolism. With a lower metabolism, your body burns less energy aka fat.

You might weight less on the scale, but you might also see loose skin around your arms. You might often feel hangry... moody with lack of energy from lack of nutrition. Instead, you need to eat what your body needs to sustain your vital organs so you can live properly.

I discovered that in the gym, everyone is focused on building leaner muscle mass while lowering body fat. Body weight is hardly important for looking slim and trim. Have you noticed that bodybuilders are heavy and yet they look trimmed and strong with a very low body fat percentage?

Which brings us to the power of water. Water is needed during the process when the body uses fat as energy. And as you might already know, water has many benefits in your body, including absorption, digestion, and secretion.

When your body is dehydrated, your energy level declines and often you overeat and eat unhealthy foods. Or you may take over-the-counter medications to mask symptoms like headaches caused by dehydration, which causes more dehydration.

Whereas, having more water gives us more energy without overeating. It's important to note, according to some findings, there are more people who die of dehydration than realized. So, get adequate amounts of water daily to support your body.

And there you have it. These are my crazy findings and discoveries in my journey from having an average looking 50 years old body to build this bikini fitness figure and I believe it is possible for you too.

About Helen Fong, CCHt, NLPP, PTT, CSC, EFT

 Helen Fong is an international Bikini Fitness Champion, Health coach and Influencer, and NLP Practitioner. With four years of experience in this field, Helen graduated from Transform Destiny with a Certification in NLP.

Helen is passionate about helping women in their 40s and 50s look and feel young again. Helen's speciality is showing clients how to get slim and trim even after 50 years old. Through her own experience, Helen can motivate and empower women to become the best version of themselves.

Helen's accomplishments include 1st, 2nd and 3rd places in multiple Bikini Fitness competitions. She is also the author of the book "TonedAt50", which shares her journey in the fitness field that 50 is the new 30.

Helen is an inspiring example of how age should never be a barrier to looking and feeling good. She is passionate about motivating and inspiring women across the world to reach their health and fitness goals.

Helen is an inspiring figure in the health and fitness industry. With her enthusiasm and dedication, she is helping women of all ages to look and feel their best.

To get Helen's gift, visit:
www.BPABook.com/gift/Helen

160

The Attitude of Gratitude

John Jaco, MSW, LSWAIC-WA, CCHt

Maintaining an "Attitude of Gratitude" is a phrase seemingly over or mis-used these days to where it has no meaning. "Oh yeah, got to be thankful!? Sure! Yeah, whatever!" Then we go on with what we were doing, anyway.

Being a therapist, whose clients have some sort of affective disorder interfering with their everyday functioning, whether with day-to-day work or relationships, this IS a big deal. Maintaining such a view is paramount to improving mental health as maintaining an Attitude of Gratitude (AOG) as well as being mindful (mindfulness) has been shown in multiple studies to be an incredibly powerful way to address what is wrong, not working, and how to overcome one's "overwhelm".

The worst thing that could happen is nothing changes/improves, or one truly DOES move forward with a sense of relief, having gained a much stronger sense of authority because you have faced that which has been holding you back for so long.

Before going on any further, we should define exactly what AOG means by simply breaking down the words. First, the word "attitude" has multiple meanings, but the one most relevant to AOG is (per Google): "a settled way of thinking or feeling about someone or something, typically one that is reflected in a person's behavior." "Gratitude" is defined as "the quality of being thankful, readiness to show appreciation for and to return kindness."

Now, if one combines these two definitions, it becomes quite complimentary: "a settled way of thinking or feeling appreciative in returning kindness to oneself or others." This shall be the working definition as we go through this chapter.

It has been my experience that when one is "stuck in stinkin' thinkin'", one cannot feel an AOG. Why? Because we have run out of solutions to what we see as problems. "I can't do X because of Y." or "If I only had X, I could accomplish Y." X and/or Y could be seen or perceived as those things we see as obstacles to overcome or things we perceive as out of reach or undeserving of our possession or accomplishment because of our entrenched "stinkin' thinkin'".

This stinkin' thinkin' feeds off itself as it has become an "uninvited guest" that refuses to leave from either shame, blame and/or guilt. The reality is we do this to ourselves as an attempt to motivate and overcome these obstacles that keep us from growing. These "problems" can be from past disappointments, unachieved goals, mistakes, failures or even successes we do not think we can ever achieve again.

By installing and maintaining an AOG, the antidote has been found. The hard part is acknowledging that you CAN change as well as maintain this view. As Wayne Dyer, PhD has said when quoting St Francis of Assisi, "we don't have problems, we THINK we have problems."

This view is powerful and is the basis of how one can truly see that problems are merely constructs within one's mind that we allow to manipulate our behavior, mood and affect. I am constantly challenging my patients to refocus and/or reframe their cognitions/belief systems once they get to the point they can believe in their own change in mindset. (I could reference many psychologists here if necessary: Carol Dweck, Judson Brewer, MD, Wayne Dyer, Jose Silva, as well as the founders of NLP if necessary, and other psychologists.)

The key to AOG is persistence. For example, I had a patient recently who said she was an avid practitioner of meditation and mindfulness. But she could not seem to shake her negative self-view of being unlovable or not good enough. This negative self-view led this patient to have sleep issues, neuromuscular pain, headaches, and a past eating disorder.

I asked her what mantra she used while in the lotus position. She said that she would repeat various phrases such as "release tension/stress now" (in various parts of her body) or "eliminate stress/anxiety".

This was, of course, FAR from being effective, let alone an AOG. So, I simply broke out my thesaurus and looked up the antonyms of the negative words she was using: Tension, stress, anxiety, etc. Interestingly, these are all feelings that we all experience, but the simple antidote to those words is the more positive: RELAX, CALM and PEACE, etc.

It should be pointed out that many only see anxiety as a bad thing/problem, but it is just that that helps keeps us safe and alert from those things that could harm us and of which allowed our ancestors to survive attacks by the dreaded Saber-toothed tiger, mama bear, or other predator who saw US as a threat.

The problem with focusing on having tension, stress, and anxiety is that we feel tension, stress, or anxiety ABOUT BEING tense, stressed or anxious. This is the point when we say, "Oh my gosh, I'm freaking out!" This creates a thought loop/spiral that could even trigger a panic attack that even bystanders can see.

What can make it even worse is the well-meaning observer who sees the distress and says, "you need to calm down!" All of this is completely OPPOSITE to AOG because one cannot even feel thankful when in a state of anxiety, stress, fear, or even a negative self-view.

The simplest solution to negative feelings once recognized is to say over and over with sincerity:

THANK YOU

This may sound silly, even hokey (Sic). But it works WITH SINCERITY and intention. You must mean it to your very core. AOG requires this attitude to be always expressed with sincerity.

The root of gratitude is grace. Which, in this context, is a verb, not a noun. It is important to understand grace in the secular context to avoid confusion. To be clear, when one refers to grace as a noun, it is defined (per Google) as "simple elegance or refinement of movement or courteous goodwill".

As a verb, it is defined as "doing honor or credit to (someone or something) by one's presence". The latter definition fits with gratitude as one expresses gratitude as grace. We see this played out in the rudimentary rituals of etiquette such as giving grace before a meal (giving thanks/being thankful). But without sincerity and intention, one does not practice true AOG in this context.

Being aware of the beauty all around you right now as you read this by noting the light that you have to read this as well as the teachers/parents/friends that helped you learn to read the words on this page and the food that nourished your body so that you have the energy to pay attention to the words being read as well as being able to interpret their meaning.

Even the temperature of the surrounding air in the spot where you are at this very moment. Notice the smells of the air or of the nearby food being cooked or the beverage you are thinking about sipping as you read this, hoping to learn something new that could propel you on your way forward with more confidence, vigor, and desire than before.

By simply refocusing onto that which you would PREFER to be attentive, you are already changing your self-view toward an AOG. Remember, the human brain cannot perceive the negative of something. I can prove it.

Do NOT think of a dog! Huh? What are you thinking of? Hopefully a cute furry one! So, NOT thinking about tension, stress, or anxiety cannot be done, so DO NOT EVEN LET IT INTO YOUR MIND! This is NOT positive thinking, rather is preferential thinking: Thinking, imagining and verbalizing only that which you prefer and want.

Hopefully, that is tranquility, calmness, relaxation, and peace, etc. For example, "Thank you for tranquility, calmness, peace, quiet, relaxation, success, desire, and instant authority."

One must consider one of the most difficult and neglected things to do is giving gratitude to yourself. Yes, I mean give thanks to yourself. Your own efforts must be acknowledged by the one who is actually putting forth the effort: YOU!

You may say to yourself, "well that sounds conceited!" Well, to anyone who is reading this thus far, you may be seeking ways in how you can be "positively awesome". If that is so, then this may be an area of deficit as it is for most people who may see themselves as "people-pleasers", going through bereavement, adjusting to a difficult period of life; have children, a stressful job, or are simply looking to better themselves in some way.

One must be sincere in giving to themselves and maintaining an AOG. Let's try it right now. Simply close your eyes with sincerity and intention repeat three times mentally or out loud softly, "THANK YOU."

And remember, your Attitude of Gratitude is the chief determinant of your success. With it, you can develop confidence, security, comfort, and authority. You have within you an ability; a gift, with which you can change any past habit as well as overcome any obstacle.

YOU can change YOU! And, the unpleasant habits and difficulties of the past? Leave them in the past, because you are determined to start new, positive behaviors, and see things differently even better than before.

Look forward to the good days coming, new experiences, new success, new understandings, and a new enthusiasm. And this new enthusiasm glows and radiates throughout you with an instant authority that will continue as long as desired.

THANK YOU

About John Jaco, MSW, LSWAIC-WA, CCHt

 John Jaco; BA, MSW, LSWAIC-WA, CCHt is a Licensed Social Work Independent Clinical Associate (Washington State) with over 30 years of experience. He holds degrees from the University of North Texas, University of Arkansas at Little Rock, in Sociology, Clinical Social Work, as well as certifications from Transform Destiny in Hypnotherapy, and Neuro-Linguistic Programming.

John specializes in helping adults between the ages of 18-108 (as we are all a work in progress) to overcome their "overwhelm" as well as anxiety and depression while providing tools to turn their struggles into strengths. He has helped hundreds of people across the United States better manage their weight, and addictions, as well as better manage his clients' emotional hurt and grief processing.

John is passionate about helping people heal, not just physically but emotionally too. He is dedicated to providing his clients with compassionate and non-judgmental care. He provides a safe and supportive environment for his clients to make the changes they need in order to move forward with their lives.

To get John's gift: A free hypnosis session: "Overcome Unwanted Obstacles", visit:
www.BPABook.com/gift/John

"We become what we think about."

Earl Nightingale

Caring For Yourself
The Surprising Link Between Self-Care and Positivity

Roselito de los Reyes, NLPMP, MTT, MHt, MSC, EFT

The first time I experienced boarding a plane was unforgettable. I was with my family, and we were going to the United States. The curious excitement was contagious as my son Karl and JP's faces lit up with joy and wonder.

I remember the captain's voice coming over the intercom, directing us to heed the flight attendant's safety instructions. And then came the part that really struck me - you know, the part where they tell you that just in case of an emergency, you have to first put on your own oxygen mask before you help your kids?

That moment of realization really hit home for me, and I felt a rush of emotions. I realized that as a parent; I had to care for myself to be there for my family. It was a powerful reminder that there would be times when I need to first take care of myself before I can take care of others.

And yet, seeing the excitement on my family's faces made it all worth it. It was an experiential journey filled with anticipation, wonder, and the promise of new adventures in a strange new place ahead. And as we soared through the clouds, I felt a sense of gratitude and excitement for the journey ahead.

171

For achieving greater happiness and fulfillment in life, self-care is one of the important things you can do for yourself. Whether taking time to meditate, exercise or engage in other self-care practices, putting your needs first is essential for maintaining overall well-being. Many people, just like me, struggle with this concept because they feel guilty about focusing on their needs.

But did you know that self-care can also have a powerful impact on your positivity and outlook on life? In this chapter, we'll explore the surprising link between self-care and positivity and how taking care of yourself can lead to greater happiness, resilience, and overall well-being.

The Basics of Self-Care

Self-care is essential for maintaining overall well-being and cultivating a positive and optimistic outlook on life. But what is self-care, exactly? According to the World Health Organization, self-care is: "the ability of individuals, families, and communities to promote health, prevent disease, maintain health, and to cope with illness and disability with or without the support of a healthcare provider." Simply put, self-care is the practice of taking care of oneself: physically, emotionally, and mentally.

The benefits of self-care are many, including improved physical health, reduced stress, and greater happiness and fulfillment. When you take time to care for yourself, you're better equipped to deal with the challenges and stresses of daily life, and more likely to feel positive and optimistic about your future.

Self-care is not only important for your own well-being, but can also affect how others perceive you. When you take the time to care for yourself, you raise your vibrational frequency and it sends a message to others that you value yourself and your needs. People who prioritize self-care are often perceived as confident, capable, and reliable.

When you take care of your physical health, you not only feel better, but you project an image of vitality and energy around you.

This can take many forms, from engaging in physical activities like hygiene, proper nutrition, exercise, or yoga to practicing mindfulness and self-compassion.

By prioritizing exercise, healthy eating, and getting enough sleep, you show others you value your health and are committed to taking care of your body. This will lead to increased respect and admiration from self and others, and can even inspire them to take better care of themselves.

And yet, many people struggle with the concept of self-care because they feel guilty about focusing on their own needs. This is where self-compassion comes in.

The Power of Self-Compassion

Self-Compassion is an essential component in self-care, and it is all about being kinder and more forgiving to *yourself*. When you practice self-compassion, you're able to deal with setbacks and failures and are less likely to get caught up in negative self-talk and self-judgment.

This is a vital aspect that is often overlooked. It is about treating yourself with the same kindness, understanding, and concern that you would offer a good friend. Many people struggle with self-compassion because they believe that being hard on themselves is the best way to motivate improvement and cause change.

Here are five ways that you can be compassionate to yourself:

1. Practicing Mindfulness: Take a few minutes each day to be present in the now and connect with your feelings and thoughts. Awareness can help you identify any negative self-talk or patterns of self-judgment.
2. Speak Kindly to Yourself: You might be surprised how often you can be incredibly hard on yourself and address yourself in a way that you wouldn't even wish on your worst enemy. The way you talk to yourself has a powerful impact on your self-esteem and overall well-being. Try speaking to yourself like you would to a very good friend.
3. Forgive Yourself: Look, we all make mistakes, and it's important to be forgiving toward yourself when you do. Acknowledge your mistakes, learn from them, and move on.
4. Practice Gratitude: Focusing on the good in your life will cultivate a sense of gratitude. This can help *shift your*

perspective towards a more positive outlook and increase feelings of self-worth.

5. Take Care of Your Physical Health: Practicing self-care by taking care of your physical health can help you feel better and increase your self-esteem. This can include eating a balanced, supplemented diet, engaging in regular exercise, and getting enough sleep.

Keep in mind that self-compassion is not about being self-indulgent or letting yourself off the hook. It's about treating yourself with the same kindness and understanding that you would offer someone else. By being more compassionate to yourself, you can improve your overall well-being and cultivate greater happiness and fulfillment in your life.

The Power of Positive Thinking

One of the most important ways in which self-care can lead to much greater positivity is through the power of positive thinking. When you focus on the positive aspects of your life and cultivate a more optimistic outlook, you're more likely to experience greater happiness, reduced stress, and improved overall well-being.

Some techniques for cultivating a more positive mindset include goal setting, visualization, gratitude journaling, and positive self-talk. By taking time to focus on the good in your life, you can help rewire your brain to see things in a much more positive light and cultivate a more optimistic outlook.

Is There a Connection Between Self-Care and Positivity?

This is a no-brainer, isn't it? While the connection between positive thinking and self-care may be clear, several organizations and researchers have found that there is a direct link between self-care and positivity. In fact, studies have shown that practicing self-compassion and mindfulness, two key components of self-care, can lead to greater happiness, reduced stress, and improved mental and physical health.

One reason for this is that when you take care of yourself, you're signaling your brain that you are valuable and worthy of care. This can lead to greater self-esteem and a more positive self-image, which can lead to greater positivity in all areas of your life. People will notice and complement what they observe, and this would create an upward spiral to improve mental well-being.

A Story of a Person I Knew

Growing up in the Philippines, Dagul had a strict disciplinarian of a mom and a dad who feared her. His mother had high expectations for him and his two sisters. She would often corporally punish him severely for even the smallest mistakes.

This upbringing had a profound impact on Dagul's personality, and he developed a mindset of always trying to please everyone before himself. This mindset was reinforced when he started school and was relentlessly bullied by his peers. He felt like he had to earn their approval and acceptance, even if it meant sacrificing his own needs and wants.

As Dagul grew older, got married, and had children of his own, he carried this mindset of people-pleasing with him. He always put others' needs first, often to the detriment of his own well-being. Dagul found it difficult to say no to requests or to prioritize his own needs, even when he was exhausted or overwhelmed. He did not realize it, but he was lacking in self-compassion. He was hard on himself, always striving for perfection, and was quick to criticize himself when he fell short.

It wasn't until Dagul started experiencing burnout in his career that he realized the importance of self-compassion. He had been working long hours, sacrificing his personal life, and neglecting his own needs for the sake of his job. It was only then, when he hit rock bottom, that he realized he needed to change his mindset.

He started practicing self-compassion by being kinder to himself, practicing meditation, exercising, forgiving himself, setting boundaries, and prioritizing his own needs. He realized that taking care of himself was important not only for his own well-being but also for his ability to be present and helpful to others.

Dagul's story is a reminder for me about practicing self-compassion in our lives. You cannot always please everyone, and it is not healthy to put others first at the expense of your own well-being. By taking care of yourself and being kind to yourself, you can better serve others and be happier and more fulfilled in your own life.

Strategies for Incorporating Self-Care into Daily Life

While the benefits of self-care are many and clear, it's challenging to know where to incorporate self-care practices into daily life. A lot of heart-centered people put their needs aside to help others first and then neglect their own needs. However, there are many practical tips and strategies that can help you prioritize your well-being and make self-care a regular part of your daily routine.

These are just suggestions, and you can take whatever you wish that would move the needle and re-read this chapter again to get another suggestion. The most important thing is to move the needle a step at a time to gain the habit of a full self-care routine.

Some tips for incorporating self-care into daily life include setting priorities, keeping a journal, practicing meditation, identifying and releasing guilty patterns, taking quality supplements, managing time effectively, and creating a personalized self-care plan.

By taking time to prioritize your own well-being, you're more likely to make self-care a regular part of your daily routine and experience the many benefits that come with it. For cultivating greater positivity and well-being in life, self-care is one of the most important things you can do for yourself. By taking time to care for yourself physically, emotionally, and mentally, you're better equipped to deal with the challenges and stresses of daily life, and are more likely to experience greater happiness, resilience, and overall well-being.

While incorporating self-care into daily life can be challenging, there are many practical tips and strategies that can help you make self-care a regular part of your daily routine. From setting priorities to managing time effectively and creating a personalized self-care plan, there are many ways you can make self-care a priority and reap the many benefits that come with it. Take one step, do one thing, and implement for a week, then add another one the following week, and so on.

In conclusion, self-care is essential to maintaining overall well-being and cultivating a positive and optimistic outlook on life. Whether taking time to exercise, meditate, or engage in other self-care practices, putting your needs first is essential for achieving greater happiness and fulfillment.

By incorporating self-care practices into daily life and cultivating a more positive mindset, you can create a foundation of well-being that supports you in achieving your goals and aspirations and living a more positive and fulfilling life.

About Roselito de los Reyes, NLPMP, MTT, MHt, MSC, EFT

 Roselito is a certified Neuro-Linguistic Programming (NLP) Trainer and Success Coach who helps individuals and small business owners get clarity on their goals and build their businesses. He believes everyone has the potential to create the life of their dreams and is passionate about helping his clients unlock their true potential and achieve success.

As a powerful advocate of personal growth and development, Roselito has a unique ability to identify the root causes of his client's problems and provide them with the tools they need to overcome them. His expertise in NLP and coaching has earned him a growing number of clients who have experienced amazing success under his guidance.

Overall, Roselito's mission is to help many people just like you become successful and achieve their dreams, by providing them with the clarity, guidance, and resources they need to create a life of success, wealth, and abundance.

To get Roselito's gift, Self-Love in Action: Acts of Self-Care ebook download, visit www.BPABook.com/gift/Roselito

Creating Awesome Teen Impact with Positive Communication

Mischa Holt, MNLP, MCHt

Teenagers are my favorite people, truly. When observed without judgment for their often outspoken or controversial opinions, there is much they can teach us about life and living. I have watched teens engage in projects that make rocket scientist look like preschoolers. Their level of depth when doing something they love allows them to lose track of time as they are immersed in their passion. This is a flow state that many adults would pay money to tap into. Yet, on the flip side, their resistance to the things they don't want to do is even stronger.

While communicating with teenagers can be challenging, parents or adult mentors can use a few simple techniques from the field of Neurolinguistic Programming (NLP) to help teens get clear and focus on what they want. This will help them shift from negative self-talk and resistance to more empowered states of being. As a bonus, these tools work with adults, too!

Effective communication is a key component in building healthy relationships. NLP offers an innovative approach to better communication, enabling adults to connect with teens on a deeper level. NLP originated in the late 1970s by Richard Bandler and John Grinder at the University of California, Santa Cruz. It combines the study of mind, language, and behavior into powerful language patterns that can help people better understand how others process and filter information.

NLP provides a model for creating an optimal communication between us and our environment to create chemistry between people, resolve conflicts, and maximize personal and interpersonal communication. Creating this atmosphere is helpful in all areas of life and allows the speaker to create a maximum impact on their conversation partners. As a parent, you can model resourceful language for your teen with positive results.

First things first, you need to understand what you are trying to achieve with your communication. Do you want them to behave better? Do you want to motivate them or change their attitude?

Then you need a strategy to accomplish your communication outcome. The easiest thing to do, yet least effective, is to use your authority as their parent to force them into doing what you want. Since it's natural for people to rebel against authority or being told what to do, you can easily see why this is the least effective strategy and where the conflict between parents and teens comes in.

When you set yourself up from a place of power, it might get you a result in the short-term, but it certainly won't do you any favors in the long-term. Instead of engaging in these power plays the real trick is to understand where your teenager is coming from. What do they value? What are their goals? What is important to them? When you start from their perspective, you are already in a much better position to connect.

You can use one of the key principles of NLP, which is understanding the importance of rapport. Establishing rapport means building a connection with the person you are communicating with. Rapport is merely a feeling of like between two people.

You can establish rapport easily by mirroring and matching the other person's physical and verbal patterns, including gestures, posture, breathing rate, and tone of voice. This helps to improve communication by creating a more comfortable and welcoming environment. Establishing rapport takes about thirty seconds to achieve when you use your body to match theirs. You know you have achieved it when you first match them and then you switch to lead them with a new body language and they follow you.

For example, they may stand with a hand on one hip and talking with their other hand, moving about. As you listen, subtly move in the same way that they move. Quickly you will notice a sense of feeling like you like each other. At this point, test leading them by moving differently, such as clasping your hands or scratching your nose and see if they follow. If they follow, you have established rapport and you can move on with your conversation easily. Rapport is subtle and powerful when influencing others.

Another key strategy when working with young people is to be careful of your own language. Get into the habit of giving them positive and specific suggestions about exactly what you want them to do as opposed to vague, negative suggestions about what you don't want them to do. We know from the study of NLP that the unconscious mind cannot recognize a negative. For example, if you say to your teen, "Don't be late," their subconscious only picks up "be late" and that is what will happen.

Instead, focus on and suggest what you want to happen. That could sound like, "Be on time returning tonight." With just a simple rephrasing of what you focus on, you get better results, and you are modeling positive language and intention for your teen. When you communicate positively in front of your teen, they are more likely to pick it up for themselves. They will do what they see you do.

Another key concept from NLP is the difference between the conscious and subconscious mind. Your conscious mind is the part you are aware of, the thinking part of you. This is where you analyze data, decide, and set goals. It can only process about seven things at a time, plus or minus two, to account for our good days and bad days.

Your subconscious mind is the realm of emotion and preservation. It takes care of things like your breathing, heart rate, and cellular health without you needing to consciously do that to preserve your body. It also takes in millions of details from the environment around you day to day. And it's where your memories are kept and it maintains all of your perceptions, learnings, and habits. Your subconscious mind is very symbolic and taps into pictures, sounds, and feelings. It is extremely powerful.

To put this in perspective, your conscious mind makes up 0.006% of your mind, while the subconscious makes up the remaining 99.994%. Wow! What if you could tap into your teenager's unconscious mind to get results?

Successful parents and influential adults do just that! They use metaphors and imagination to communicate with teenagers on a subconscious level. Metaphors bridge the gap from the conscious to the subconscious, allowing learnings and positive resources to be readily accepted by the receiver without lecturing or being told what to do.

Metaphors can be scripted or intuitive and should be based on the teenager's preferences to give shape and color to their own emotional world looking through the eyes of another. This generates a working environment in their mind that allows for the legitimation of varying emotions, lessons, and outcomes. Their own subconscious mind will search for the meaning most relevant to them and their desired outcome.

Let's look at an example, shall we? This metaphor is simple and only takes a minute to present. I've used it with hundreds of students.

I hold up a pencil or stick and tell the group to imagine it's a bone. If I'm standing in front of a dog and I wave the bone in the dog's face side to side and then toss the bone a few yards away, what will the dog do? "Chase the bone," the group yells back. But what if I'm standing in front of a lion? I wave the bone in the lion's face from side to side and then toss it a few yards away. What will the lion do? "Eat you!" is often the response from the students.

The fact is that the lion may eat me. The lion could eat me. But there is a fundamental difference between the mind of the dog and that of the lion. The dog has tunnel vision and sees beyond the bone. It becomes simple: If I control the bone, I control the dog's reality.

Of course, it's different from the lion. The lion sits upright as I wave the bone, eyes looking beyond the bone and directly at me. The lion has poise, understands that the bone is just a small piece of a larger prize. He has more control over himself, more autonomy. The lion can go after the bone. He can sit there and stare at me. He can eat me.

The "bone" is like our experience when anger arises. When I'm angry, what type of mind do I employ? Is it the dog's mind or the lion's mind? What about when I am extremely anxious? Am I chasing the bones of worrisome thoughts or sitting with autonomy like the lion?

Sometimes we can get caught up in the bones of our own stories, thoughts, images, sensations, and emotions. By remembering the image of the lion sitting there poised and present, non-reactive, we notice the state of mind we are trying to cultivate with mindfulness. Not relaxed, but present, non-reactive and non-judging. Autonomy to face whatever "bones" are thrown our way.

I often follow up this metaphor with a discussion about what "bones" apply to their life presently. This makes the metaphor real and applicable to them. And then, without teaching, I just ask to let that question sit in the space between us as their subconscious mind makes its own connections to the places that tempt them and the mind they choose to employ. It points toward the symbol of the dignified lion. I then use the lion's mind terminology as a language thread in future conversations to bring their awareness quickly back to their own choices and resources.

When I check back in with students during struggles, I can say, "What mind were you in? The dog mind or the lion mind?" And they understand exactly what I'm talking about.

The metaphor of the Lion Mind to describe mindfulness comes from Larry Rosenberg's book, *Breath by Breath.* I invite you to collect metaphors you can use with the teenagers you influence. Help them think and use their minds to connect to positive internal resources and connections.

Now you have three tools that you can use immediately to impact the teens in your life: rapport, modeling positive language to focus on what you want, and metaphors.

Now it's up to you to play a little. Use these techniques and see what results you get for yourself. Tweak your actions to get more powerful results each time.

Learn a little, do a little, repeat... forever! Enjoy connecting.

About Mischa Holt, MNLP, MCHt

 Mischa Holt is a self-directed education advocate and the owner of Mind Oasis Education. She has twenty-five years of experience mentoring families that chose non-traditional education paths. Mischa is passionate about helping teens and parents build connected, empowered relationships by unlocking their true potential to create the life they desire.

Now a clinical hypnotherapist in Marietta, Georgia, she specializes in parent-teen communication and family relationship coaching. Through hypnotherapy, she guides her clients to better understand their internal struggles and how best to overcome them. She helps her clients make rapid, lasting changes in their lives in order to achieve a greater sense of well-being and joy.

Mischa is the best-selling author of *Unschooling Teens: Simple Strategies to Conquer the Overwhelm of Getting Your Kids Through High School*. In her book, she shares insights and strategies on how to empower teenagers to create their own paths to success and launch them into their next life adventure after high school.

To get Mischa's free Hypnosis Recording, *Communicate Better with Your Teens*, visit:
www.BPABook.com/gift/Mischa

"Once you start replacing negative thoughts with positive ones, you'll start seeing results."

Willie Nelson

Emotional Drunkenness: The Hidden Consequences of Sleep Deprivation

Elizabeth Garvey, CCHt, NLPP, EFTP, TTP, CSLC

With so much to do and so little time, it is easy to view sleep as a hindrance rather than a vital component of daily life. However, sleep is important. In fact, getting enough sleep can supercharge your performance, both personally and professionally. Let's explore the power of sleep and how it can help you achieve your goals.

First, proper sleep can bring a wide range of benefits to our lives. For instance, it can enhance our emotional regulation, which can lead to better decision-making, more stable moods, and reduced stress levels. It can also play a significant role in managing chronic pain, as it promotes healing and reduces inflammation.

Second, for productivity and motivation, sleep can be a game-changer. It can improve our ability to focus, make connections, and solve problems, allowing us to perform at our best. Overall, prioritizing sleep can help us lead healthier, happier, and more fulfilling lives.

Let's look deeper into a couple of these areas since persistent lack of sleep can cause severe health problems and affect your overall well-being.

The most obvious consequence is being tired and groggy the next day. This can affect your performance at work, your relationships with others, and your overall quality of life. But

191

it's just the tip of the iceberg. Being sleepy can be like driving under the influence of drugs or alcohol. Your reaction times are slow, decision-making abilities are weak, and it compromises your coordination when sleep deprived.

Studies have shown that being awake for 18 hours straight can lead to the same level of impairment as having a blood alcohol level of 0.05%. And if you stay up for 24 hours, it's equivalent to a blood alcohol level of 0.10%, which is over the legal limit for driving in many states.

Everyone knows the consequences of driving under the influence, and most people would never consider getting behind the wheel after drinking or using drugs. Yet, many don't think twice about getting behind the wheel when sleep deprived. This can endanger everyone on the road.

This is a type of *sleep induced drunkenness*, but there is another type that's just as serious. I call it *emotional drunkenness*. It's that feeling you get when you're so exhausted that everything seems a little off, doesn't it? Your brain becomes less able to regulate emotions, which can lead to outbursts of anger or frustration. And it's more difficult to manage stress, anxiety, and other negative emotions too.

This affects your relationships, doesn't it? For example, if you often snap at your loved ones and business associates or overreact to minor irritations, it can create tension and conflict. This can erode trust and lead to the breakdown of those relationships.

Also, it's hard to recognize and respond to the emotions of others when sleep deprived. This can make it more difficult to empathize with others or understand their perspectives, which can also lead to tension and conflict.

Please keep in mind, emotional outbursts due to sleep deprivation are not a character flaw, but a symptom of a larger issue. When you take steps to improve your sleep habits, you can reduce the likelihood of emotional drunkenness and improve your relationships with others.

You can also improve your professional productivity and performance. When you're well-rested, you're more focused, alert, and able to concentrate. This means that you're better able to solve problems and find creative solutions. But sleep deprivation can lead to decreased cognitive function, decreased motivation, and decreased productivity. In fact, studies have shown that sleep deprivation can lead to a 30% decrease in productivity. That is significant!

Along with productivity, sleep is also essential for learning and memory retention. Your brain processes and stores the information learned throughout the day when you're sleeping. This means that getting enough sleep can help you learn more efficiently and remember more effectively. Without enough sleep, your brain struggles to process and keep information, leading to decreased learning and memory performance.

Not to mention, proper sleep can help you be more creative. Your brain is active, processing information and making connections while you rest. This means that your brain can continue working on problems and projects even when not actively thinking. Many famous inventors and creative geniuses, including Thomas Edison and Salvador Dali, have credited sleep as an important part of their creative process.

I know, this is a lot to think about, isn't it? And I haven't even touched on the critical biological processes that happen when sleeping. Those are important too, as those processes regulate weight management, cortisol, and growth hormone management, and chronic pain management.

Chronic pain is a big issue, right? The relationship between chronic pain and sleep is a bit like the chicken and the egg. On the one hand, chronic pain can make it difficult to fall asleep, stay asleep, or get the deep sleep that your body needs to repair and recharge. This can lead to increased pain and discomfort during the day.

On the other hand, lack of sleep can also exacerbate chronic pain. When sleep-deprived, your body produces more inflammatory markers, which can worsen pain and inflammation. In addition, sleep is important for helping heal and recover from injury or illness, so when you don't get enough rest, it can be harder for your body to manage chronic pain.

So, if you're suffering from chronic pain, it's important to pay attention to your sleep habits and try to get the rest your body needs. This might involve developing a bedtime routine, creating a comfortable sleep environment, or even talking about potential treatments for chronic pain or sleep disorders. By addressing both chronic pain and sleep together, you may break the cycle and improve your overall quality of life.

Let's look at a great example of how I helped a client improve the quality of his life. Tony Mazza reached out to me on LinkedIn. He was struggling with anger and had found my profile. Tony wanted to know if I could help.

I set up a call with him and we talked about how he was angry all the time and it was affecting his relationships. I could hear the pain in his voice as he described the effect his anger was having on his family, whom he loved dearly.

So, I explained emotional drunkenness to him, and I asked him questions about his sleep habits. It was then that he shared he really hadn't had a full night's sleep since discharged from the Army National Guard in 1968, *five and a half decades ago*! I told him to schedule an appointment as soon as possible.

The first step was to get Tony sleeping again, so we focused on sleep hypnotherapy. I did a complete assessment of what was keeping him from sleeping and integrated that into his session. It absolutely amazed him how great he felt when he came out of the light trance forty minutes later. It was like he had just woken up from a full night's rest, which is a common statement from my clients after hypnosis.

The next day, I got a call from Tony. He had slept a full night for the first time since 1968. So, I had him wait a couple of weeks before seeing me again so he could integrate his new sleep cycle. He quickly started seeing a difference in his ability to regulate his emotions. Best of all, so did his wife and grown children.

From there, we worked on triggers of anger and tools for managing his emotions. One trigger was that Tony was a serial entrepreneur and was running four businesses, two of which he did not enjoy, but he thought he needed the income and did not see how he could retire. Mind you, Tony was already in his seventies.

So, I gave him assignments to get clarity on his income, resources, and then helped him adjust his efforts so he could release the businesses he did not love within a couple months of beginning work with me. The time he saved in not running two of those businesses made more time available for his grandchildren and other activities he loved.

Just by getting his sleep back, we began healing his family dynamics, changed the outlook of his professional life, and create time and space for him to enjoy his grandchildren more. I still hear from Tony several times a year and he's always excited about the direction his life has taken.

When I reached out for permission to include him in this book, he quickly responded with, "Of course it's okay, you changed my life!"

It's moments and responses like his that encourage me to keep working with veterans and help to give back some of the freedom they fought to secure for all of us. While my focus is helping veterans, everyone can benefit from my programs.

So, let's look at some sleep hygiene basics to help you sleep better now. The National Sleep Foundation recommends that adults aim for 6.5-9 hours of sleep per night. Keep in mind that everyone's individual needs can vary. Some people may need more sleep, depending on their age, activity level, and overall health. The key is to pay attention to your body and listen to what it's telling you. If you're tired or groggy, it's a sign that you may need more sleep.

Of course, getting enough sleep isn't always easy. With busy schedules, late-night work projects, and other distractions, it's hard to prioritize rest. Here are five simple steps you can take to make sleep a priority:

1. Establish a bedtime routine: Create a routine that helps you wind down and prepare for sleep each night. This could include things like taking a warm bath, reading a book, or listening to calming music.
2. Create a comfortable sleep environment: Make sure your bedroom is dark, cool, and quiet. A supportive mattress and comfortable bedding will help.

197

3. Avoid caffeine and alcohol: Both caffeine and alcohol can interfere with sleep, so it's best to avoid them in the hours leading up to bedtime.
4. Turn off electronics: The blue light emitted by electronic devices can disrupt your sleep cycle, so it's best to turn them off at least an hour before bedtime. It's even better to leave them outside the bedroom to charge.
5. Stick to a schedule: Go to bed and wake up at the same time each day, even on the weekends. This can help regulate your body's internal clock and make it easier for you to fall asleep and wake up.

By making sleep a priority and incorporating it into your daily routine, you will get many benefits and enhance your performance. But sleep issues can run deeper than setting the stage of good rest, though. Sometime other factors like emotional distress and chronic pain can keep you from optimal sleep.

That's why I recommend everyone who struggles with sleep to get a sleep analysis done. It only takes 30-60 minutes to unpack your sleep routine and identify problems to resolve, and like Tony, it could set the stage for a complete life transformation.

Once we identify those problems with your sleep cycles, we can use hypnosis to change habits faster and remove stress and anxiety that may keep you up at night. It can also help you relax and release any negative thoughts or feelings that may contribute to your sleep issues.

So, if you're struggling with emotional drunkenness or sleep issues, please remember that you're not alone. These issues affect a significant percentage of the population, and I have many resources available to help you overcome them quickly and confidentially.

About Elizabeth Garvey, CCHt, NLPP, EFTP, TTP, CSLC

 Elizabeth Garvey is a Clinical Hypnotherapist and Sleep Coach at usleepnow.com. She is passionate about helping veterans finally sleep, sometimes after decades of insomnia.

Elizabeth graduated from Transform Destiny with Board Certifications in Hypnotherapy, NLP, EFT, TIME Techniques, and Life Coaching, and is currently working towards Master Certifications. She is also a professional writer, editor, and artist.

Elizabeth's lifelong commitment is to assist others. She is driven by her own experiences as a daughter of a Vietnam Veteran. Furthermore, she has successfully battled and recovered from PTSD in her adult life, and her passion for supporting veterans stems from this. Her intention is to employ her skills and know-how to provide veterans the help they require, getting the rest they deserve, and establish a life they adore.

Elizabeth does this by creating personalized plans that fit each veteran's needs. She is dedicated to making sure her clients are comfortable and safe throughout their journey so they can reach their goals and thrive in their post-military life.

To get Elizabeth's gift for you, visit: www.BPABook.com/gift/Elizabeth